Dancing With The Ten Thousand Things

Dancing With The Ten Thousand Things

◆

Ways to Become a Powerful Healing Presence

Tom Balles

iUniverse, Inc.

New York Lincoln Shanghai

Dancing With The Ten Thousand Things
Ways to Become a Powerful Healing Presence

iUniverse, Inc.

For information address:
iUniverse, Inc.
2021 Pine Lake Road, Suite 100
Lincoln, NE 68512
www.iuniverse.com

ISBN: 0-595-31160-1

Printed in the United States of America

To my mother and father
Ruth Ann and Bernie Balles
who gave me everything

The potential for healing exists
in each one of us
in every moment
in every role we play
in every relationship we have
in every conversation that takes place
and in every profession and institution we serve.

Contents

WITH GRATITUDE

I offer a deep bow of gratitude to the following teachers with whom I have been blessed throughout my life.

To Oscar Ichazo and members of the Arica community, who helped me begin cultivating an internal observer. That alone is the gift of a lifetime.

To the wonderful T'ai Chi Ch'uan teacher, Benjamin Pang Jeng Lo, who ended every class with a warm smile and the simple words "more practice." Ben, I am still practicing.

To the late Dr. J.R. Worsley and Dr. Judy Worsley, for dedicating their lives to nourishing the spirit of Chinese medicine.

To Pere Claude Larre, the late founder of the French branch of the Ricci Institute. Thank you for revealing the beauty of the Chinese wisdom traditions.

To Fritz Smith and Jack Daniel, who were among my first acupuncture mentors. Your words of wisdom still ring in my ears.

To Merijane Block, who insisted that I write. Your speaking changed my life. I am glad you are alive to read this book.

To Jenny Josephian, John Kirkwood, Susan Leahy, Devi Brown, and Keith Stetson—in Five Hands Clapping you created a space in which I recovered my creativity.

To Bob Duggan and Dianne Connelly, who for more than 30 years have tended the growth and evolution of the Tai Sophia Institute for the Healing Arts in Maryland. Thank you for living your promises.

To Julia Measures and John Sullivan, who embody virtue and the expression of Large Mind. May this work serve our common life.

To Katherine Johnson, Tom Payne, and Cheryl Walker, for being faithful friends, colleagues, and collaborators. In your presence, all of my work gets richer.

To all the patients, students, and faculty I have been fortunate enough to work with over the last twenty years. Your passion and courage remind me of the importance of writing this book.

ACKNOWLEDGEMENTS

A number of friends helped shepherd this book to publication:

Early on in the writing, my friend, Mary Heckman, called me back to the bigger book waiting to be written.

Kevin Meddleton and Samantha Berg gently reminded me to write in the voice I use while teaching.

Elise Hancock brought to my first two drafts a wonderful combination of toughness flavored with compassion.

The gifts of the five phases and the pointers about embodying them (Chapter Eight) were gathered with my delightful colleagues, Karen Greenstein and Tori Hovde.

My wife and best friend, Nancy, offered insights that created substantial changes in the structure of the book.

John Wilson took took the words *simple*, *warm*, and *inviting*, and transformed them into a beautiful cover design.

Henry Chan of Photo Gallery in Columbia, MD produced the photo for the back cover.

PREFACE

Apropos to a work of non-fiction I want to share the influences that specific individuals and communities have had on the creation of this book. Several streams of thought have been brought together to shape a distinct and coherent philosophy of healing.

For twelve years (1973-85), I was an active participant in the self-realization work of Oscar Ichazo and the Arica Institute. Oscar was the first spiritual teacher I came across who spoke unequivocally about the unity of life and of humanity being One. To this day, when doing spiritual practices, I use the beautiful invocation from that time, "I offer the results of this work for the benefit of all of humanity…"

Through his various trainings, I began the work of cultivating an internal observer. The work of the Arica school also included body-based practices to assist in staying aware throughout the day. My growing interest in the body naturally drew me to the practices of yoga, T'ai Chi Ch'uan, and Aikido. Over time I learned the importance of daily, embodied practice and came to understand the use of the whole body as an instrument of healing.

I began my acupuncture studies in 1982, and in 1985 participated in an acupuncture seminar offered by the French sinologist, Pere Claude Larre, and an American acupuncturist, Peter Eckman. Father Larre was enchanting. He spent most of the first morning speaking about a single Chinese character he had drawn on the board. Through him, I had my first glimpse of the breadth and depth of the Chinese wisdom traditions. The use of numbers as symbols and the organizing principles of One, Two, Three, Four, and Five employed in this book are loosely adapted from his writings. I take full responsibility for my creative use of them. Were he still alive, I would hope Pere Larre would forgive me my youthful folly.

Through studying an approach to acupuncture developed by the late Doctor J.R. Worsley and Dr. Judy Worsley, I came to know what a powerful teacher and partner Nature can be. Their teachings continue to inspire me after two decades of practice.

The most recent and recognizable influence has been my association with the Tai Sophia Institute for the Healing Arts in Laurel, Maryland. I was a senior faculty member in the Master of Acupuncture program from 1996-2002 and served as Dean of Faculty from 1997-2001. Currently I hold the position of Distinguished Lecturer and teach in SOPHIA (School of Philosophy and Healing in Action) and the Institute's Masters degree program in Applied Healing Arts.

Some linguistic distinctions I use come out of the SOPHIA program, offered by the Institute since 1987. Were some of these distinctions first made by my colleagues John Sullivan or Julia Measures? Dianne Connelly or Bob Duggan? I offer my regrets if proper acknowledgments have been omitted.

The material in this book evolved from ten years of classroom teaching, workshops, and public presentations on two coasts. The experience of working with thousands of patients, students, and acupuncturists serves to remind me that we are all teachers and learners. From the original root of the word educate (e—out, ducere—to call, bring, or lead), I have learned how to call others out in the classroom and the treatment room; to bring forth the collective wisdom available in each other's presence. I hope this book also serves to call *you* out, to participate fully in life as it shows up around you.

INTRODUCTION

Each day calls us to tend life beyond ourselves. *Dancing with the Ten Thousand Things* speaks to those who answer the call and yearn to be a more powerful healing presence in the world. This book will help transform your care and compassion into effective action.

You *already* are a healing presence. In the back rub you offer your child, the extra time spent with a discouraged partner, the depth of listening offered to an upset co-worker; you are tending life beyond yourself. You already carry all that you need in your being.

Imagine taking the gifts and skills you already possess (and may not be aware of) and amplifying them. What you may now do unconsciously you will come to do with awareness. Being a healing presence is a way of life that will become second nature to you.

The text outlines the journey of waking up through being of service. In working with the material, you will observe two changes taking place: you will experience less unnecessary suffering and greater possibilities in the life you share with others.

The distinctions and practices that make up the book can be applied to your self, family members or friends, life in the workplace, in organizations, and in community life. Although you may not end up saving the world, you will learn to consciously tend to life one moment at a time.

Becoming a powerful healing presence takes time and practice. There are three steps you can take to maximize your learning:

First, adopt beginner's mind. Similar to using any new tools, your first efforts may be clumsy. There will come times when you want so much to help yet everything you say or do makes matters worse. You just know you are off the mark! Be kind and forgiving to yourself. Have courage. You are a beginner. Continue practicing and you will grow in skillfulness and confidence.

The second step in embodying the learning is writing down your experiences. Buy a journal to use as a practice log at home and another small memo pad you can carry around with you. Write at least one paragraph each day about what your practice was and what you observed in response. Be faithful in your commitment to practice and write. Words have power. Use them to document your progress.

The third step is to invite others along for the ride. The book takes you on a worthwhile and rewarding adventure. Form a small group and commit to talking or meeting once a week about your observations and practices. You will learn faster this way and share in the joys of discovery. Knowing that you will be speaking to others will boost your commitment to be in practice.

A great deal of substance lies hidden in the simplicity of the writing. Take your time moving through the book. Taking on the practices will help you embody the distinctions. At different moments, you might sense that the text is just the tip of the iceberg and feel there is much more to learn. You will be correct. Each chapter could be a course in itself. Opportunities to learn and practice these distinctions in community are available through Tai Sophia Institute for the Healing Arts and elsewhere. (See Resources) At the very least I hope to provide you with new questions to ponder and new conversations in which to be engaged.

◆   ◆   ◆

The notion *being of service* goes by many names: helping out, making a contribution, having an impact, making a difference, love, and compassion. Whatever you choose to call it, contributing to the well being of others is an essential component of a meaningful life.

I would like to offer a working definition:

A healing presence cultivates
distinct ways of being, doing, and speaking
that serve life and the lives of those around them.

Let's explore the definition further.

"cultivates distinct ways"

Choose to set aside your childish ways. No longer do you think "I'll be however I want to be…do whatever I want to do…say whatever I want to say." A willingness to be of service is the sole requirement for being a healing presence: the willingness to be and do and speak in ways that forward life.

"of Being"

Philosophy constitutes the ground of our being. As used here, the word *philosophy* refers to the love of wisdom. Your philosophy; the core values, principles, and paradigms from which you operate will be challenged in this book.

Cultivating awareness is a way of *being* common to many spiritual and wisdom traditions around the world. Part of your work will be to cultivate an internal observer capable of making distinctions between the phenomena of life (i.e. your **per**ceptions) and your stories and conclusions about life (i.e. your **con**ceptions). In cultivating an internal observer, you will develop a keen eye for the way your words and actions affect others.

Being a healing presence means *being present* to all of life, exactly as it shows up, pleasant or not. Parts of the journey may open and soften your heart. You will become more sensitive to the presence of pain in yourself and others.

One final aspect of being is the willingness to *be* what life asks us to be. In one moment life requires that you be still and listen, in the next moment to stand firm, in the next to simply make a cup of tea. What would it be like to tend to life in whatever form it shows up?

"Doing"

To be a healing presence requires practice, a word I use both as verb (as in practicing the piano) and noun (to have a practice). This book offers you practices you can take on for an hour, a day, a week, a month or a lifetime. They can be applied across many domains from our intimate relationships to leading international organizations.

Choosing to listen and not interrupt others is an example of a simple practice. Pointing to what's possible is another. These practices are not a "once and done" phenomenon—you will fall off the horse at some time or another! Through practice, your philosophy comes alive in the world.

A second facet of effective *doing* is recognizing the many ways you can understand and respond to any situation. This book teaches time-tested ways to live with intention and purpose; to live your life from choice. No longer will your life just happen. You will choose—if not what happens, how you react.

A final aspect of *doing* is the ability to take effective action in the world. As you hone your presence you will find your good intentions springing to life transformed into actions that powerfully touch others.

"and Speaking"

Language may be the most underrated of the healing modalities. The words we use, the conversations we are in, the questions we ask, and the stories we tell greatly impact our lives and the lives of those around us. For example, when recreational drug use by teenagers is labeled a problem, disgrace, blight, or epidemic, we look for solutions that will wipe it out, make the problem disappear. When the same phenomenon is described as a wake-up call, opportunity, or opening, then we may look for new ways to communicate with our children. Different words call forth different worlds.

Blending what you say with how you say it gives potency to language. Sections of the book will teach you how to maintain congruency of your voice, posture, gestures, and touch. A powerful healing presence speaks with the whole body, each and every part sending the same message.

"that serve life..."

Marriages, families, friendships, workplaces, institutions, and communities are all living systems. In the text I treat them as living things, a metaphor you may find useful. I also encourage you to explore the possibility that each of these entities literally has a life of its own. Throughout the book, you will find ways to be a powerful steward in each of these domains.

"and the lives of those around them."

In serving others, you come to know yourself more deeply. Genuine service stands in contrast to conspiring with, enabling, or being a martyr to others. Your health and well-being are not separate from those who live and work around you.

You will know over time that you are becoming a more powerful healing presence when life *around* you starts to show up differently. Life will flow more smoothly, with less effort, and less unnecessary suffering.

◆   ◆   ◆

Chapters One through Three introduce you to some basic ways of being, doing, and speaking that comprise a healing presence. Chapters Four through Eight expand the practices while firmly grounding them in a philosophical framework. This framework has its roots in the Chinese wisdom traditions—yet rest assured you need not be familiar with these traditions in order to receive the full benefits of this book. Chapters Nine, Ten, and Eleven expand the practices even further by applying them to life in a body, life in community, and life in conflict.

Each chapter consists of short essays that use examples and teaching stories to anchor distinct principles. The focus, however, is on how *you* will make these principles come alive in the world. Each essay contains *Reflections* that allow you to explore your current ways of being, doing, and speaking, and *Practices* that can be applied to all the domains of your life.

Even if not always mentioned by name, God, love, faith, and hope are woven into the fabric of any book written about healing. Through this work, I hope you embody a deeper connection with all of life, and come to recognize that we are One. It has always been so and will always be so.

1
WAYS OF BEING

Awareness happens for everyone when there is the interest and readiness to be in touch directly, immediately, without description, or explanation or diagnosis. When there is intimate touch with what is happening right here, this moment, without any separation.

—Toni Packer
The Light of Discovery

Imagine three interlocking circles representing our Ways of Being, Ways of Doing, and Ways of Speaking. The image demonstrates that how we *be*, what we do, and what we say affect and are affected by each other. Consider these examples:

My thoughts about John affect how I interact with John and what I say about him.

(way of being)   (way of doing)   (way of speaking)

Working with John will affect my stance towards John and what I say about him.

(way of doing)   (way of being)   (way of speaking)

What I say about John affects how I work with him and my opinion of him.

(way of speaking)   (way of doing)   (way of being)

I use the word *being* to describe internal states: our feelings, thoughts, attitudes, stances, postures, beliefs, and moods. Noticing our internal state is the first step in our capacity to change it. In turn, changing our internal state can quickly and effectively change our actions and speaking.

Chapter One explores some of the distinct ways of being that comprise a healing presence. These essays will introduce the notions of *being present* and cultivating an internal observer. In them you will find distinctions between perceiving life and conceiving life, and a comparison between Small Mind and Large Mind.

STAYING AWAKE

Come back to this moment. Life is unfolding right now. Bear witness to all the joys and sorrows.

What would you say is the most challenging human activity? Telling the truth? Loving other people? Making a living? Programing the VCR? I say that living in present tense sits right up there among our difficult challenges. Paradoxically, it is amongst the most rewarding of activities. This manner of being, common to many spiritual and wisdom traditions throughout the world, goes by many different names: being present, having an observer, wakefulness, awareness, mindfulness, bearing witness. Cultivating your capacity to be fully present lays the foundation for being a healing presence.

When fully present, you are aware of how life is moving both inside and outside your skin. Awareness includes the sensations of pleasure and pain, hot and cold, mental and emotional states, and the movement of energy, blood, and fluids throughout your body. Full awareness brings you alive to the infinite phenomena arriving from outside your skin—all that you see, hear, smell, taste and touch.

Being present requires the capacity to self-reflect, to step outside yourself and to shine the light of awareness back on yourself. When present, you can be angry and be aware of your anger, think a thought and be aware that you are thinking, wash the car and know you are washing the car. Being present focuses your attention on this moment, how life is unfolding here and now. Watch closely and you will quickly see your tendencies—how often your attention is drawn to rehashing experiences from the past and speculating about events in the future.

When being a healing presence, your internal observer also monitors how others receive you. For example, I make sure to watch my students as I teach. Are their eyes meeting mine? Are their bodies turned towards me or away? Are they slumped in their chairs or at the edge of their seat? When I sense I am not being heard, I change some aspect of how I am presenting myself so that a new connection can be established.

To be present is to bear witness to life just as it is. You accept all the joys and sorrows, all the wonders and terrors, while fully acknowledging what is so. A healing presence chooses to stay present even (or perhaps especially) when it is uncomfortable to do so: your co-worker has begun drinking again, your good friends John and Sally are getting divorced, your teenager is having unprotected sex or was found doing drugs.

Again we run into paradox; the single greatest source of both our suffering and our achievements is the desire for life to be different than it is. Bearing witness by no means implies inaction, passivity, or approval. We can and do bear witness in our actions and our speaking. Acknowledging a learning disability, for example, is the first step in working with it. Child abuse must be identified before steps can be made to halt it. That a conflict exists must be acknowledged before there can be movement towards conflict resolution.

Being a healing presence is a *both/and* phenomenon; having the courage to acknowledge what is so and taking steps to ease any unnecessary suffering.

Reflections

When are you uncomfortable experiencing what is happening inside your skin? How do you respond? How else might you respond to the discomfort?

Where in your life do you keep your senses open and stay connected with whatever is going on around you? At home, at work, in the garden...

In what situations do you tend to close down, to isolate and separate yourself from life? How else might you respond in those moments?

Practices

Create a period of time each day in which you return to your senses. Sit quietly and notice what is arising in you (thoughts, feelings, movements) and around you (sights, sounds, smells...) Write a few lines in your practice log to describe what you perceive.

If disturbing thoughts and images tend to linger, (regrets, worries, fears) write them down in your practice log. Take a moment to acknowledge that your thoughts are often quite different than the *truth* or what is *real*. How does this practice affect the impact of your thoughts and images?

For a distinct period of time (a day, a week) make it your practice to observe how others receive you. How do family members, friends, and co-workers respond when you are speaking? Do they meet your eyes? Do they turn toward or away from you; shift their posture or the look on their face? Note your observations in your practice log. Whenever you sense you are not being heard, ask yourself how else you might be with them.

PERCEIVING AND CONCEIVING

Be aware of when you perceive life and when you are conceiving it. Choose
stories in which there is room for all to breathe, to grow, and to thrive.

Have you ever been concluded by another person to *be* a certain way before
they have even gotten to know you? Have you been prejudged or labeled as being
rude, cold, quiet, or pushy? Do you sometimes sense that a person is responding
to you from an inaccurate story they have created about who and what you are?
Most of us find the experience quite painful.

Essential in being a healing presence is to know the distinction between when
we observe life and when we create life, when we **per**ceive life and when we **con**-
ceive life. As you will see, not knowing the difference may increase the potential
for pain and suffering.

By "perceptions," I mean the many phenomena we receive directly from our
internal and external senses. Our "conceptions" are the many stories, conclusions,
comparisons, abstractions, interpretations, and generalizations that arise around
our perceptions.

For example, apple as perception (phenomenon) occurs when I pick an apple
up from the table. I see its shape and color, smell its fragrance, feel its texture, and
sense its weight in my hand. I take a bite, hear the crunch, and taste the subtle,
changing flavors.

By apple as conception (story), I mean the many comparisons, interpretations,
conclusions, questions, and generalizations that arise with the phenomena:

> *I really like eating apples.*
> *I wonder if this apple has pesticides on it?*
> *This apple wasn't as good as the last one.*
> *I wish there were more apples so I could bake a pie.*
> *This was the last apple, maybe I shouldn't have eaten it.*
> *And so on…*

You can work with any object, being, structure, process, and event as perception and conception, phenomenon and conclusion. You can perceive "father"
and you can conceive "father". You can hold "marriage" as phenomenon and
"marriage" as conclusion.

Any stories you might create about apples would be relatively harmless. The
conclusions you create about yourself and others, however, can get tricky. Often

our conclusions isolate, separate, restrict, and encumber. This is what I mean by unnecessary suffering.

Note how the following stories limit the possibilities of how life might show up:

> *Rita is no fun.*
> *Jack is never going to change.*
> *I'll never be any good at this.*
> *This new class is a problem.*
> *My child is faking a belly-ache.*
> *My boss really hates me.*
> *Getting old is really a bitch.*

From a singular moment or event, we often conclude others and ourselves to be a particular way. We forget we created the story and then proceed to fix it in stone. We turn our story into a permanent "thing", a "truth", and act accordingly. Our story often becomes a self-fulfilling prophecy.

Of course, it is impossible to make no conclusions, create no stories. Creating stories, assessments, and conclusions is critical to human life. It is what our minds do and thankfully so. While stepping off a curb, for example, I want to be able to conclude that I should jump back—that large yellow object **is** a school bus bearing down on me! The mind will always conclude something about every phenomenon. The challenge is whether our conclusions are going to serve life and the lives of those around us.

As each story arises, can we recognize it as a story? Then we can consciously pick and choose among stories, adopting those stories big enough for others and ourselves to live in. Our stories will forward life and open up new possibilities for what can take place.

Note how the new stories below create a little more breathing room for all.

Old Story	New Story
Rita is no fun.	I haven't found out what Rita likes to do.
Scott is never going to change.	I'll try interacting with Scott differently.
This new class is a problem.	This new class is an opportunity.
My child is faking a belly-ache.	I'll ask my child how she feels about school.
I'll never be any good at this.	I need help in learning how to do this.

My boss really hates me.	*I'll ask my boss why she's mad.*
Getting old is really a bitch.	*It's time to go back to my yoga class.*

Chapter Three will expand the notion of story and explore ways to heal the narratives that define our lives.

Reflections

What are some of the stories you have created about yourself? Are they spacious, empowering, filled with possibilities? If not, how might you rewrite them?

What stories about yourself do you hold as being "the truth"? What would it be like to hold them as a "maybe"? Can you see situations in your life where the story is not true?

Practices

Take a few inanimate objects (a book, your computer, the desk) and write about each one first as a phenomenon. Describe what your senses tell you about the object. Then write down your conclusions and stories about the object in your practice log. Ask yourself what your stories reveal about you.

Make it your practice to catch yourself when you are making stories—while driving to work, attending a staff meeting, or during an evening out. Articulate the actual phenomena. Check to see whether your stories and conclusions help to move life forward.

Reflect on a person whom you have concluded to be a particular (unpleasant) way. Would a different story give them room to show up differently in the world? Write down several new stories about the person that give them room to breathe. Use this practice with those whom you struggle to get along.

Pick an event in the future that you have already imagined will "be" a certain way (a difficult conversation with your boss, a phone call with a friend who is struggling). Make a practice of creating three new stories of how the event might unfold. Write them down in your practice log. After the actual event, take note of how life showed up differently than you had first imagined.

MOVING BEYOND SMALL MIND

Keep a close eye on the movements of your mind. Cultivate your internal observer day by day. Lay the groundwork for living from choice.

Staying awake includes paying attention to the workings of our minds. During the course of any given day it appears as if we actually have two minds and that we move back and forth between them. One mind is the mind of the younger, the immature, growing person in us. I call that Small Mind. The other mind is that of the elder, the mature, wise person in us. I call that Large Mind. (Others might prefer using the words ordinary, everyday, or local for "Small" mind and transcendent or global for "Large" mind.)

The columns below are mirrors with which to see the responses of Small Mind and Large Mind. Can you see yourself in both of them?

When in Small Mind I...	When in Large Mind I...
Tend to be closed, hard hearted, exclusive	Tend to be open, warm hearted, inclusive
Speak about faults and shortcomings	Speak about strengths and gifts
See in black and white	Am at ease with contradictions and ambiguity
Am oppositional	Am cooperative
Think in terms of obstacles, barriers	Think in terms of possibilities, opportunities
See problems "out there"	Examine my own choices, responses, attitudes
Am quick to blame, justify and defend	Am accountable and responsible
Give power away	Retain and use power
Create separation and isolation	Create connection and partnership
Create false hopes, talk a good game	Create clear expectations, embody humane conduct
Am imprisoned	Am free to choose
Am asleep	Am awake
Suffer more	Suffer less

What I Sound Like

When in Small Mind	**When in Large Mind**
I have to	*I choose to*
I can't...it's hard to	*I'm a beginner at*
He/she/made me	*In his/her presence I notice that*
That's just the way I am	*I tend to...I usually respond by*
There's nothing I can do	*I'll look at other options*
It's always going to be the same	*I'll see what happens this time*
What's wrong? What's the problem?	*What's possible?*
It's not my fault.	*I'll see what I can do*

The phrases *being in reaction* and *losing our observer* are synonymous with *being in Small Mind*. In other words, Small Mind concocts a whale of a story about yourself or others that leads to more suffering.

For example, my latest experience of being in Small Mind took place only hours ago. I had an appointment to meet my wife and look at a house that was for sale by the owner. I was quite excited because Nancy had previously driven by this property and said it looked like quite a find. But the owner wasn't there. After waiting for fifteen minutes, we decided to call. Only then did we discover the owner had gotten tied up and couldn't meet us for several hours. Not only that, his house was not the one we were salivating over, but the fixer-upper next door!

I was quick to blame Nancy for making an error, quick to judge the owner who hadn't called us. Indeed, I fell into opposition to the whole process of buying a house. I was ready to chuck the whole idea.

Notice how all my problems were *out there* and how I allowed the situation to take away from the joy of experiencing a crystal clear fall afternoon. Talk about being imprisoned!

What can you do when you recognize yourself stuck in Small Mind? The first step is to acknowledge that is where you are: cutting yourself off, closing down, blaming others, and suffering like crazy. The second step is to imagine what operating from Large Mind would be like and take steps to manifest it. Acknowledge how you have been responding to the situation, choose another response, and jump back into the process.

As much as we may resist the notion, whether we come from Small Mind or Large Mind is a choice. Shifting from Small Mind to Large Mind is similar to exercising different muscles in a new workout routine. The more you do it, the easier it becomes, and the less you suffer. It is encouraging to know that every time you are able to shift from Small Mind to Large Mind you are building a stronger foundation for living from choice. Having choices means having power. Which mind will you keep on choosing?

Reflections

In what situations do you tend to be most reactive and respond from Small Mind, (i.e. speak about other's faults, are quick to defend yourself…)?

What would a response from Large Mind look like instead?

Where in your life are you not operating from choice? How can you shift to Large Mind in these arenas?

Practices

Practice listening for Small Mind and Large Mind. Sit in a public place and listen to the conversations going on around you. Can you hear Small Mind speaking? Large Mind? Write down what each mind sounds like.

Take a situation where you feel in opposition to a person or group of people. What are the phenomena? What conclusions have you made? What would cooperation look like in this situation? Take a step in the direction of cooperation.

Each day for a week, practice taking on different qualities of Large Mind. For example, on day one practice speaking about people's *strengths and gifts*. On the second day, focus on *possibilities and opportunities* instead of problems and barriers. On the third, *savor ambiguity and contradictions*. Each day write a few lines in your practice log describing how life is showing up differently.

2

WAYS OF DOING

The key word for our time is practice. We have all the light we need; we just have to put it into practice.

—Peace Pilgrim

From some initial examples of Ways of Being, let's move along to Ways of Doing: the external actions we take in the world. Chapter Two begins the conversation of how to translate your care and compassion into effective actions in the world; regardless of whether you are sitting around the kitchen table, conversing with friends, attending a staff meeting, or leading a community organization.

The first piece explores the surprising similarities between the roles of a shaman, an actor, and a healing presence, and will challenge you to shift your normal levels of expression. The second essay focuses on recovering the use of touch in everyday life. The final two essays introduce the notion of practice, how to create a practice for yourself, and tips on how to keep it lively.

AN ACTOR, A SHAMAN, A HEALING PRESENCE

*One moment requires firmness, so you stand firm. Another moment calls for a light touch so you inject humor. A third moment is solemn, so you **become** awe and respect. Your ability to touch others grows and matures. Like the consummate actor and the skillful shaman, you become a powerful presence in your own right.*

For many years I resisted the metaphor expressed by Shakespeare in *As You Like It*:

> *All the world's a stage*
> *And all men and women merely players.*
> *They have their exits and entrances;*
> *And one man in his time plays many parts.*

Life is serious business I would think to myself, not something to trivialize. Through years of listening to my patients' stories in the treatment room, I came to realize there are many similarities between how we participate in daily life and the work of an actor.

The shy young woman, for example, transforms into a mesmerizing teacher to her third grade students. A father cooing over his baby morphs into the enforcer with his older son. The cool businesswoman striding home from work becomes a hungry and passionate lover. While the core of who we are remains constant, our exterior resembles a chameleon. We change our costumes, masks, persona, and dialogue to fit in with the unfolding scene.

Attending theater was a part of the prescribed regime at the ancient Greek temples of healing. Just as they do today, actors evoked and amplified the full range of emotions in order to touch and move their audience.

In many traditions, the medicine people or shamans do the same through their rites and rituals. They employ voice, posture, gestures, and touch to create a shift in the consciousness of the patient. To emphasize their similarities, consider whether the following characteristics are true of a compelling actor, a skillful shaman, a powerful healing presence, or all three.

> *Engage our imagination and create powerful visions.*
> *Perturb our sense of what is real.*
> *Share their vulnerability and reveal hidden aspects of themselves.*
> *Open our hearts and communicate at deep levels of being.*

Call us to wakefulness and a sense of connection.
Rekindle the spirit of community.
Are understanding and deeply empathetic.
Transform into something/somebody else while working.
Embody distinct qualities of spirit and inspire participants.
Are held in awe by the community.
Make visible and manifest that which is normally hidden.
Communicate with forces that lie beyond our normal senses.
Convey power through their ways of being, doing and speaking.
Take risks for the sake of participants.
Use their entire body as instruments in their work.
Embody paradox, ambiguity, and contradiction.

A healing presence learns to transform their compassion and good intentions into effective action. Over the years, I have watched hundreds of students studying to be acupuncturists learn to amplify their intentions, extend themselves, and transmit distinct qualities of being to others. Not unlike an actor or shaman, students practice intentionally calling forth and *being* joy, empathy, understanding, respect, courage, vision, direction. They do so when their patients forget that they too can access and call forth these qualities when needed. These students learn not just to insert a needle; they learn to *be* the needle.

With practice, you can also learn to be the needle. Chapter Eight will guide you in employing your voice, posture, gestures, and touch to powerfully convey your intentions to others—be they a spouse or partner, a child, friend, or co-worker.

As Shakespeare wrote, each of us in our time plays many parts. The love and compassion at our core gives rise to the willingness to be what is needed, do what needs to be done, say what needs to be said.

Reflections

Where in your life do you put on a good show?

What components in that setting engage you so fully (the audience, the script, trying on a different mask)?

Are there moments when you transcend yourself, go beyond the normal boundaries of your identity? What are you doing when that happens?

How do you communicate with others at the deepest levels?

Are you willing to reveal different parts of yourself for the sake of those around you?

Practices

Take a day and practice shifting your normal level of expression by 10 to 20%. Whether telling a joke, giving directions, offering sympathy, or acknowledging someone, take it slightly over the top <u>or</u> decrease the wattage from your normal ways of expression. Explore what it is like to amplify or decrease your presence. How did life show up differently?

Sometime during the next week place yourself at the center of a conversation or discussion. Be willing to be in the spotlight. Speak with the intent of touching and moving those around you. Write down in your practice log what you learned about your capacities.

Practice transmitting a conscious intention: In this conversation, I will convey my sympathy. In this meeting I will be respectful. Were you successful in transmitting your intention?

Take advantage of opportunities during the week to express yourself non-verbally. Learn to be a silent presence. Let your eyes, facial expressions, gestures, posture, and touch express your intentions. Record your observations.

RECOVERING THE USE OF TOUCH

Touch is one important way to transform your intentions into action. Expand the qualities of touch that you now use. Learn to use touch as an effective instrument of healing.

A profound depth of connection can be generated solely through touch. In my acupuncture practice, I grasp the hands of my patients in order to read the energetic pulses at the wrists. Over the years I have seen that simple gesture produce sighs of relief and tears of sadness, provoke waves of fear and stir up ripples of laughter.

We use touch in our daily life to communicate emotions, amplify our intentions, and ground our verbal expressions in another person. A firm grasp of the shoulder prevents a child from bolting into the street. A playful pat or a tickle can signal rising passions. A supportive touch on the arm conveys empathy and understanding. A light and respectful touch acknowledges the grieving of a friend.

Physical touch may be the single most powerful method of healing living creatures. More than any other means, touch expresses our willingness to be with another no matter what. Through touch, we see and are seen, hear and are heard in ways not available through the other senses. Touch can succeed where verbal communication falls short; sometimes only touch can reach your terrified child, disheartened partner, or despairing friend. Touch provides direct contact with the place that hurts, a gesture that in itself begins the healing process.

The list of different kinds of touch is long and each form of touch conveys a different intention: pats on a child's head, athletes' slap on the butt, a gentle stroking of your lover's cheek. Hugs vary just as much from Hollywood air kisses, to stiff A-frame hugs, bear hugs, and the intimate hug of a sexual partner.

Depending on the situation, the use of physical touch may be impractical, inappropriate, and even illegal. For those reasons I hold the opportunity to touch another person as truly a privilege. Some people consider any kind of touch in a social situation to be presumptuous and yes, some people simply do not like to be touched. At the same time, the benefits of using touch greatly outweigh the risks of being rejected. If someone does not appreciate your touch, rest assured that you will know: they will tense up, cross their arms and legs, or turn away. A simple apology will suffice.

Someday, perhaps all those wishing to be health care practitioners will learn the skillful use of touch as part of their training. Maybe there will also come a day when our children will be taught healing touch, as well as safe touch. I hope so. It behooves us to reclaim touch as an instrument of healing.

Reflections

In what arenas of your life is physical touch appropriate?

How many different kinds of touch do you give? How many do you receive?

Where are there opportunities for touching that you are not taking advantage of?

Practices

Practice increasing the frequency with which you initiate touch—with your partner or spouse, family members, or friends. Record the changes you observe in your practice log.

Add touch to amplify your intention—be it to get someone's attention, offer sympathy, give instructions, ask a question etc. Write down the responses you received.

TAKING ON A PRACTICE

To be a healing presence is to be in practice. Consciously take on ways of being, doing, and speaking that contribute to life.

The root of the word practice comes from the Greek praktikos—to be distinct from the theoretical or ideal, disposed to action rather than speculation, something that becomes visible through action. To practice is to acquire proficiency and competence, to move from being a beginner to becoming adept. Similar to being present and cultivating an internal observer, having a practice (of prayer, meditation, or worship) is at the heart of many spiritual and wisdom traditions around the world. That sense of practice is enlarged here to embrace the work of healing.

I use the word practice as both verb (practicing) and noun (having a practice).

A good practice is a stretch—it takes you beyond your normal comfort zone. Like all of us you can expect to fall off the horse every once in awhile and forget you even have a practice. A practice is not a "once and done" phenomenon, it is cultivated over time. Ironically a practice is not about self-improvement or making you a better person. It is about tending to life. You will discover that a good practice will call you to wakefulness and life beyond yourself.

Over the last few years I have asked participants in my classes and workshops to create simple practices they will take on as they leave the programs. Here are some examples:

I listen and do not interrupt others.
I choose Large Minded responses.
I point to what's possible.
I bring humor, laughter and lightness.
I give advice only when asked and only once.
I use people's names when I speak to them.
I create quiet time in my day.
I am attentive to how I use my words.

A practice is a big enough gesture to make a difference and concrete enough to know that you are doing it. A practice is practical and portable. It is something you can do at home, with friends, and in the workplace. You can choose to take on a practice for a day, a week, a month, or a lifetime. The practices at the end of each chapter will help you embody the written distinctions found in the text.

Some of them may just start to show up regularly in your life. Then the distinctions can truly begin to live in you.

Being in practice is different than doing good deeds. It is a choice taken on voluntarily, not done out of duty or obligation. Having a practice requires that your internal observer be in place so you can observe what you say and do, and then how life around you shows up differently. A practice requires taking a step, no matter how small; to be accountable for the life you share with others.

Use the notion of practice to extend the range of good habits that help to move life forward. More is not necessarily better. Hold practice as a gift, freely given, to those whom you touch every day.

Reflections

What practices are already in place in your daily life?

What practice could you take on that would forward the lives of those around you?

What would it look like if each of your family members took on a simple practice that would serve the life of your family?

Practices

Whenever you notice yourself feeling especially happy, comfortable, or effective, practice looking around you. Is how you are feeling related to a practice someone else has taken on—the enthusiasm of your house guest, a helping hand extended by your boss, a co-worker including you in a social event…?

Choose one of the practices from the above list and consciously work with it over a period of a day or a week. How did life show up differently? Write down your observations in your practice log.

POLISHING YOUR PRACTICE

Take steps to keep your practice lively and challenging. Let your daily practice keep you on your toes—alive and awake in the world.

How do you choose a practice that will forward the life that is unfolding around you? One starting place is to ask your friends, family members and co-workers what *they* think would be a good practice for you. Although this idea might sound daunting, I encourage you to have these conversations. You will hear some surprising (and usually helpful) responses. Less daunting would be to recall some of the phrases you commonly hear your friends and family directing at you:

> *Pay attention...*
> *Lighten up...*
> *Slow down...*
> *Get serious...*
> *You're always whining...*
> *Stop blaming everybody...*
> *You're so negative...*
> *You're always creating problems...*

Each of these phrases can be transformed into a daily practice that you can use in any setting. Again, it is important to remember that a practice is not primarily about self-improvement (although that may happen). Your intention is to have life around you show up with a little less suffering in it for all.

We can feel very enthusiastic when taking on a new practice. Often the first results are startlingly good ("That was so thoughtful of you.") Over time, however, the excitement can wear off and motivation wane. There are several ways to keep your practice alive and moving.

Who Benefits?

Identify who (other than yourself) benefits from your particular practice. Acknowledging that others will also benefit from your efforts strengthens your commitment and spurs you on when you wobble. We all know people who have made difficult changes—like stopping smoking—only after recognizing that their behavior caused others (like their children) unnecessary suffering.

Partnership

Ask someone close to you to be your practice "buddy" and have him or her check in with you on a regular basis. People who care about you will be happy to offer you their support and might even want to adopt a practice of their own!

Steps/Form/Timing

Begin with a simple practice that requires few steps and takes only a small amount of time and effort. Be specific about what the practice is and how it will show up. If your practice is to bring humor and lightness to a particular domain, how will you do so? Will you tell one joke a day? Send funny e-mails? Wear a clown nose at staff meetings. .?

Embodiment

If possible, anchor the practice with a specific phenomenon *in* your body, e.g. I will take a breath and…. I will sit down and….I will listen first, then…

Reminders

A good reminder is anything that works for you—something that will reliably grab your attention at some time during the day. Simple can work: a photograph above the sink, a Post-it note, a pebble in your pocket, wearing your watch on the other wrist. Physical phenomena are also great reminders—any shortness of breath, butterflies in the stomach, tightness in the throat—all can be used to call yourself back to awareness. Some people anchor their practices to something in the outside world: every time I place my hand on the door to my office, I think of one more thing to be grateful for in my life.

Check In

Set a specific date on the calendar when you will check in with yourself. On that day, decide whether you want to continue with the same practice or change its form. You might also declare that your practice has borne fruit and move along to create a new practice in another part of your life. Successful practices tend to stay with us, turning into new and constructive habits.

Keep A Log

Keeping a practice log accelerates your learning. One paragraph each day is enough to anchor in how the day unfolded. Be specific about the moments when you were in practice. What did you see, hear, and feel in response? How did life around you show up differently? Writing down your observations will often reveal the next practice you will adopt.

Reflections

Did your family and friends zero in on a particular habit or trait? You may want to start there.

Do you have some resistance to taking on a specific practice? If so, start small. Could you commit to adopt a specific practice for just an hour? Yes? Would you be willing to make that commitment? Yes? When will you begin? (How about now?)

Are there any costs to you and those around you by *not* taking on a particular practice? What are they?

Practices

What would it be like if co-workers took on the same practices for the sake of your common work: we will be on time for meetings; we will clean up after ourselves in the staff kitchen. How might it change the morale and climate in which you work? What would it take to create some interest? Take a step in that direction this week.

This time you create a practice to take on for a specified period of time. Walk through the guidelines above to polish your practice before you begin. Record your experiences in writing each day.

3

WAYS OF SPEAKING

There are three things of which we can be relatively certain. We are here. We are here together. And there will come a time when that is no longer so. What is the conversation worth having in the meantime?

—Dianne Connelly

Surely you can remember a time when you were powerfully moved by the words of another. Whether it was a parent's words of love and support, a teacher's words of wisdom, those of a religious leader, or powerful public persona—words are a powerful force for movement, transformation, and change.

And, the other side of the coin, words can also suppress the healthy movement of life. They can prevent transformation and forestall change.

How we speak about the world shapes both our internal states (Ways of Being) and our actions (Ways of Doing). Chapter Three invites you to a greater awareness of the role language plays in creating our world.

WORDS HAVE POWER

Talk is not cheap. What you say matters. Honor the power of words and their impact on those around you.

However abundant in our lives, words never lose their ability to touch and move us. Words possess intrinsic power. We become excited by a lover whispering in our ear, are saddened by an ailing parent's voice on the phone, or start fuming after the boss' tirade. Words can teach, guide, encourage, inspire, reassure, and unite.

Words can also destroy visions and dreams. They can tear apart relationships that have taken years to build. At times, we withhold our words from one who is starving to hear them. We use words to taint that which others hold precious and dear. Words can terrify and paralyze.

We create life and destroy life through our speaking. We can choose to build a heaven or construct a hell. Thoughtful and thoughtless words change the course of lives.

Words are the voices of time. There is no past, only what I say about it. The present is what I declare. The future is not separate from what I say it will be.

I had a terrible childhood.
It's going to be one of those days.
There's no way I could learn to do that.
I'll never be the same.
I'm not letting anybody get close to me again.

Words are symbols and metaphors, shorthand and abstractions, attempts to give name to a reality we may never fully know. Behind a single word or phrase lies a whole world of meaning. To one person the word "depressed" means he is having daily crying jags. To another, "depressed" means she has *only* been able to work 50 hours a week. A third person uses the word to encapsulate that he hasn't gotten dressed or left the house for three days. Everywhere, and all the time, it is essential that we explore each other's words to discover the unique phenomena that lie beneath them. Note how little is revealed in these generic phrases:

I'm really stressed out.
I feel like I'm going to die.
My heart is broken.
This is really weighing on me.

> *It's all downhill from here.*
> *Really, I'm O.K.*

Words have power. Words give power. Words take power away.

> *I trust you.*
> *You can do it.*
> *Tell me what I should do.*
> *I can't do anything about that.*
> *You only have six months to live.*

Words are creative and generative, opening doors to new possibilities.

> *What else is possible here?*
> *What would happen if...*
> *What are you learning from "x"?*
> *What does this remind you of?*
> *How else could we look at this?*

Words are animated and alive. They have and convey heart and soul.

> *She's an angel.*
> *It was a revelation.*
> *He lost faith.*
> *She stole my heart.*
> *I want to be together the rest of our lives.*

Words are harbingers of separation and violence.

> *You have to do it this way.*
> *You're either for us or against us.*
> *You're going to have to learn the hard way.*
> *There's going to be a price to pay.*
> *Take it or leave it*
> *It's now or never.*

Are words precursors to illness and disease? What is the impact of how we speak about our bodies and our selves?

> *That just kills me.*
> *I'm a nervous wreck.*
> *I'm out of my mind.*

I can't stomach this.
I'm sick and tired of....
This anger is eating me up.
This is tearing me apart.
I'm dead on my feet.
That makes my blood boil.
This is going to be the death of me.

Reflections

Whose words do you remember from years ago? Were they encouraging, hurtful, healing? What has been the impact of those words upon your life?

Does it serve the lives of those around you when you say whatever you want, whenever you want?

What are you teaching when you speak?

The last time you were upset and in reaction, how did others respond to your words? Was your speaking effective?

Practices

Write down the following questions on a small piece of paper and keep the paper with you for a few days. When you are conversing in a group (family members, friends, co-workers), keep these questions in mind.

Does it serve for me to talk right now?

What is my purpose in speaking?

What words would forward the lives of those around me?

When I do speak, are my words landing? Are they being received?

Are others around me opening up or closing down?

LISTENING FOR THE GREMLIN

Keep your ears tuned for the voice of the Gremlin. Take care to create conversations that keep life moving forward.

At times, we seem possessed by a mysterious creature that speaks with great authority about our life. In his book, *Taming Your Gremlin*, Richard Carson describes this creature as the Gremlin.

Sometimes we hear the Gremlin's voice coming from inside:

> *Yeah but.*
> *It's really hard to.*
> *That won't work...*
> *I don't have the time to...*
> *I tried that already...*
> *I'm not very good at...*
> *I don't have the money.*

This creature seems quite determined to keep us exactly where we are in life. The Gremlin hates change. It's rationale is subtle, yet oh so powerful! The voice of the Gremlin often gets confused with common sense.

Sometimes we hear the Gremlin speaking through others around us:

> *You can't do that...*
> *That's not like you...*
> *That's too risky...*
> *It will take too much time...*
> *You'll probably mess it up...*
> *Who do you think you are?*
> *You don't deserve to...*

Even more mysterious, sometimes **we** become the voice of the Gremlin for others:

> *That's not how I'd do it.*
> *When I was your age...*
> *It's too late for that.*
> *That won't do any good.*
> *Just leave things the way they are.*

It doesn't matter where the voice of the Gremlin comes from; the important task is to recognize its voice. With practice, you will develop a keen ear and then you can begin to reduce its power.

One approach is to call the Gremlin by name, thank it for sharing, and send it on its way. Another approach is to take the Gremlin's words, twist them, and turn them upside down. As you do, so the Gremlin will often recede to the shadows. Here are a few examples:

The Gremlin	Turning the Gremlin upside down
You can't do that.	I can do that and I might even be good at it.
That's too risky.	Yes it is risky. Maybe it's time I take a risk.
You'll probably mess it up.	I'm willing to make a mess for a while.
Yeah but.	What am I willing to do here?
You're not any good at "x".	I am willing to be a beginner at "x".
That won't do any good.	What would serve here?
You didn't do it perfectly.	You're right, I didn't—I'm a human being!

Try as we might the Gremlin does not disappear once and for all. It is quite persistent. Choosing to fight with the Gremlin will be a losing battle. Of necessity we must learn to dance with this lifelong partner. The better we learn to dance the more we retain our power to choose.

Reflections

How do you recognize the presence of the Gremlin—does it have a color, a shape, a particular feel or tone of voice? Do you notice a particular sensation in your body when it speaks?

In what areas of your personal life does the Gremlin speak most loudly—around relationships, your skills, career, income?

Where in your life do you mistake the voice of the Gremlin for the truth?

Where do you hear yourself acting as the Gremlin for other people?

When the Gremlin is really persistent, how can you respond so that life keeps moving forward?

Practices

Listen for the voice of the Gremlin in conversations. What did it sound like speaking through yourself or others? Write down what you heard in your practice log. Keep building a list of the Gremlin's favorite sayings.

Get together with a good friend to draw pictures of Gremlins. Use speech balloons just like in the comic strips to help you capture their favorite phrases: "Fat chance." "No way." Take the words and play with them—amplify and exaggerate them until they sound ridiculous. Do you see some new possibilities as the Gremlin recedes to the shadows?

Who represents the voice of the Gremlin in your family dynamic or work environment? What does the Gremlin have to say in these situations? Create some clever ways to point out the Gremlin's voice to others. How does acknowledging the Gremlin change how life shows up in these environments?

HEALING CONVERSATIONS

Each day offers dozens of opportunities for healing via the words you share with others. Know the power inherent in conversation and discourse.

All day long we swim about in an ocean of words. Clearly the Gremlin is only one voice among many that we hear. From dawn to dusk we use language to exchange information, make requests, share thoughts and feelings, create plans, ask questions, and tell stories. Our words exchanged become conversations and within conversations lay opportunities for healing.

There are a variety of conversations in which we participate, several of which have a distinct tenor or tone:

Dead-end conversations are heavily burdened with worn-out stories about ourselves and our personal gripes, complaints, and criticisms. Often these conversations revolve around our unsolicited opinions about what others should be doing with their lives. They include the litany of all that we feel is wrong with the world and what other people should be doing to fix it. Sound familiar?

Dead-end conversations travel in circles and lead nowhere. They deaden the soul.

Termite conversations are of the same family, only they occur in the workplace, where we share complaints about fellow workers, the management, the company, the organization.

Termite conversations chew away at the foundation of institutions and rarely result in any effective action.

Generic conversations are our feeble attempts to take large groups of diverse people, structures, and events and boil them down into a single abstraction or "thing". They offer us the false comfort of believing we "know" who or what we're talking about. In these conversations, for example, all Republicans (homosexuals, Catholics, Japanese, etc.) are alike, family values means the same thing to everyone, and all of us share the same feelings about the events of September 11, 2001.

Generic conversations shun complexity, ambiguity, and paradox.

Healing conversations are full of aliveness and possibility. They tend to address the present or future and participants both speak and listen—a process not as common as it used to be. In its purest form, the depth and quality of listening actually shapes the speaking.

For example, years ago while practicing acupuncture in San Francisco, I took a walk around the block with my colleague, Khosrow. I was very dissatisfied with major aspects of my life that morning and Khosrow had noticed that I was particularly vexed. As we set out he simply asked, "What's going on?" For the rest of our time together I talked and he listened. The depth of his listening allowed me to go deeply into myself to discover what was there. As I spoke I heard my own words echoing back to me. Within 24 hours, I knew I would be leaving San Francisco. In 45 days, I had moved to the East Coast.

Many conversations of a personal and professional nature begin with an assumption that something in the other (or the world) needs to be fixed. So, in lieu of listening, we fix: suggest, advise, correct, cajole, reframe, teach, and a host of other activities.

A better starting point might be to simply listen.

Is it even possible to listen freshly to another as if we have never heard this person speak before? Can we listen without comparing what this one says to what another has said? Can we listen without thinking about what we are going to say in response?

What if we declared ourselves beginners at listening? In doing so, our conversations would become healing conversations. In them we would make room for everyone to breathe and grow and contribute. Participants would share a commitment to speaking and listening. No one's speaking would be discounted.

Over time the culture of any group becomes defined by the conversations and discourse that take place within it. If you would like to bring about a change in the culture of your family, neighborhood, school, work environment, institution, government, or nation I offer a single, radical principle: **change the conversation.**

For example, I am committed to redefining the word health, and changing the culture of health care in this country. When patients first come to see me for acupuncture treatment, I reassure them that I will soon be asking about the specific concerns that brought them to my office. I choose not to start into a conversation about their symptoms. I begin instead by exploring all that is going well in their lives. I ask "Where is life is really flourishing?" and then I listen.

Within the first five minutes, my patients, like Dorothy in the *Wizard of Oz*, know that they are not in Kansas anymore. I offer them the possibility of care that embraces all of who they are—in wellness and illness, in dying and death. I engage them in a conversation that is brimming with possibilities about how they might care for themselves. One patient at a time I, and others like me, are redefining health and changing the culture of health care.

Reflections

Where in your life do you participate in dead-end, termite, or generic conversations?

Have you found they result in effective actions?

How would you instead create healing conversations with your family members, friends, and co-workers?

Are you willing to be a beginner at listening? How will you learn to listen more deeply?

Practices

For a set period of time observe what your tendencies are in conversations other than listening (i.e. advising, correcting, fixing, reframing, teaching, etc.) Then "just" listen. How were the conversations different? Anchor your observations with some notes in your practice log.

When in conversation, practice staying silent and attentive for an extra half-beat longer than usual before you reply. Notice how often the other person has more to say. Write down what you learned in those moments.

Identify a change you would like to make in the culture of a group around you—your family, the workplace, the neighborhood, and your community. How would you change the conversation that takes place there? Take a step this week to change the conversation and record your results.

THE ART OF INQUIRY

Be courageous. Ask the questions begging to be asked. Ask big questions. Skillful inquiry builds partnership.

There are only three ways to end a sentence in the English language: with a period, exclamation point, or question mark. This reflects the fact that in conversation we are making statements, voicing our assertions, or asking questions. Skillfully blending these modes of expression creates powerful connection with others.

The potency of questions reveals itself in the direct and simple queries of a child, "Mommy, why are you crying?" "Daddy, are you mad at me?" "How come we never see Grandma anymore?" Good questions reveal, guide, discover, confirm, motivate, and inspire. They engage our emotions, stimulate our thinking, provoke memories, and excite our imagination. Skillful questions reveal the care and concern of the questioner and permit new ways of looking at the world.

The principles below will assist you in using inquiry as a tool for healing.

Why, What, and How

Why questions tend to move people to explain or defend themselves. It is not uncommon for the other person to feel attacked or blamed, as *why* questions sometimes reveal our unfavorable opinion of another's actions. Take note of how you feel in your body as you read these questions.

> *Why are you going out with Judy?*
> *Why did you go back to school?*
> *Why did you buy that car?*

What and *how* questions speak to process—discovering the other person's experience and responses to life. *How* and *what* questions are open-ended. They keep the conversation alive and moving. Do these questions feel more inviting to you than the previous ones?

> *How are you getting along with Judy?*
> *What is it like being back in school?*
> *How is your new car working?*

Past, Present, or Future?

Be clear about your intention in asking a question, including what time period you are asking someone to address. Do you want to know what has gone on in the past, what is taking place now, or what will go on in the future? Conversations about yesterday, last week, last year, or ten years ago do serve a purpose. They help us to integrate and give meaning to our lives. Conversations about the present and the future are also essential to the healing process. In them we identify the terrain around us, and develop guidelines for the journey ahead.

Note how each of these questions calls to a very different place inside the person who will answer.

> *What was it like growing up in New York?*
> *What do you enjoy about living in New York?*
> *How long do you see yourself living in New York?*

Imagine for a moment a world in which we only spoke about our lives in the present and the future tense. Would it change how we identify ourselves? What questions would we ask of each other? What kind of world would we create together?

Skillful inquiry creates partnership

In some conversations, a hierarchy of roles leads one person to assume the mantle of know-it-all, as we often see in relationships between parent/child, teacher/student, boss/employee, physician/patient. By contrast, questions level the playing field. Skillful questioning places both parties on the same side, the same team, looking freshly at a given phenomenon.

For example, in my teaching it would be easy (and tempting) to create a climate in which I am the teacher, you are the student. I have the answers and you do not. Instead, I often answer questions that students pose by folding their questions back on them. If they ask what I would do in a particular situation, I ask, "What would *you* do?" No longer is there one expert or authority in the room; we are a room full of colleagues teaching one another. When treating my acupuncture patients, I often ask what they would say if they were sitting in my chair as practitioner. Their counsel and suggestions to themselves are profound and moving.

Any of our grand pronouncements and *shoulds* spoken as mother, father, teacher, boss, or health care practitioner can be turned into questions that invite exploration and help all participants to find their words. Skillful questioning helps people find their own way. Resolution of difficulties becomes a co-creation as in these examples:

> *Do you see a pattern here?*
> *Can you tell me more about that?*
> *How would you describe what's happening now?*
> *What do you think we should do?*
> *What would happen if?*
> *What would it feel like to?*
> *Where do we go from here?*
> *What do you think is the next step?*
> *What would it look like if?*
> *Have you ever had an experience like this before?*
> *What did you do that helped you at that time?*

Note how the word "we" naturally shows up more frequently in these questions, further enforcing the notion of partnership and teamwork.

"I don't know."

The most exciting time in my classroom and treatment room is when I have asked a question and a person says, "I don't know." In that moment, the student or patient is perched on the edge of discovery. Rather than ask another question I pause, as what the person says next is often a revelation. Give people time and space to access deeper parts of themselves. The pregnant pause will give birth to a discovery well worth the wait.

Consider using touch

In Chapter Two, I mentioned that it is impractical, inappropriate, and even illegal to physically touch another in certain situations, and that some people don't enjoy being touched. At the same time, a light touch while asking an important question will help a person take in your question. For example, using touch can create a powerful connection when asking a young child about a lie, asking a partner how they are really feeling, or asking a friend about getting laid off. Physical touch communicates our willingness to be with the other in these challenging situations.

Making requests

Requests are distinct questions that show up in all our relationships. The inability to make clear requests and to respond to them truthfully causes an extraordinary amount of human suffering.

If we look underneath most of our complaints, lo and behold we will find a request—a passion *for* something to be different. Any complaint or concern can be transformed into a request of another. Good requests are specific to the here and now or speak to the future. For example, "You never want to do anything…" can transform into "Wouldn't it be nice to see a movie tonight?"

In responding to requests, a simple practice is to say yes, say no, or make a counter-offer. Responses to the example above could include:

> *"Yeah, that's a great idea."*
> *"No, I'd really like to stay home tonight."*
> *"I have to finish some work—how about tomorrow instead?"*

Requests that go unanswered can become grist for even more stories, many of which are inaccurate.

Ask big questions

In the last chapter, I gave the example of how I shift the culture of health care by creating a bigger conversation with my patients. I suggested that one way to change the culture within distinct domains (family, neighborhood, workplace) was to change the conversation. Now I want to add a second radical principle. If you want to change the culture: **change the questions being asked.**

Challenge the certitudes of the existing culture. Do family vacations always involve a trip to another locale with different activities? How is our collective stance in the West towards dying and death affecting health care costs? Is punishment an effective response to crime given that our prison population has swollen to over 2,500,000 inmates? What are the bigger, deeper questions waiting to be asked in any domain?

Reflections

In what arenas do you assume a role of authority or expertise, as parent, or older sibling, or in the domain of work? In these roles, how can you create partnership through the skillful use of questions?

Where in your life are you not asking a question that needs to be asked? Where are you not asking a big enough question?

Practices

The next time a person seeks your guidance or counsel, practice folding the question back on them, exploring what they are thinking and feeling about the direction to take. See if you can turn any good suggestion you might have (a statement) into a powerful question they can investigate.

Ask questions that point to people's thoughts and feelings about the present or the future:

> *How do you feel about that now?*
> *What can you do about that?*
> *What else is possible here?*

How did these questions change the conversation? Record your observations.

Pick a relationship that appears to be stuck—a family situation, a rough patch with a friend, a struggle with a co-worker. What new questions might change the culture of that relationship? Ask those questions and record how life showed up differently in response.

Practice the art of making requests this week. Focus on making clear requests and responding truthfully to requests from others using a simple yes, no, or counter-offer. What changes do you notice?

REWRITING OUR PERSONAL STORIES

How you tell your personal story—to yourself and others—makes all the difference in the world. Choose the most compelling perspective possible. Live the most powerful story you can.

The human soul goes starving in a literal world. To live on phenomena alone would reduce us all to skin and bone. We need the meat of story to live on.

For twenty years I have had the extraordinary privilege of listening to people tell the stories of their lives. Over that time I have concluded (as have other professionals) that often the stories need healing before the person can heal. One person might tell a story of childhood abuse as a preface to "my life as victim..." Another tells the same story as an epic struggle of courage, survival and forgiveness. Which kind of story is big enough to live in, would you say?

Each of us has stories to tell and it is essential to our well being that we have a chance to tell them. Telling our stories is one way we uncover values and create meaning in our lives.

Our personal stories are a fascinating blend of real and imagined lives. There is truth in the events: my mother did die, my girlfriend did leave, and my melanoma was removed. The stories however, are largely a blend of fact and fiction. We make them up. They arise out of memory, which is highly selective and incomplete.

Take any powerful story—good or bad—from your past: the day you won (or lost) the big game, the first time a lover came to you (or left you), the moment you heard that your father had cancer. Some details are retained while others are forgotten. Some details are embellished and exaggerated, while others are denied, repressed, and discounted. We fill in the blanks with our imagination. We shape our stories to fit the image of who we believe we are. This is true not only of the past, the telling of today's events over the dinner table will already contain a good dose of fiction.

Our stories become a little more believable each time we tell them. We act "as if" and "as though" our stories are true. Ironically, that's how Joseph Campbell described myths: tales that offer us powerful teachings when we read them "as if" and "as though" the events actually took place.

Look more closely and we are likely to find that the script and the characters (including yourself) are continually changing over time. You watch in horror as the knight in shining armor transforms into a snake in the grass. You married the beautiful young princess not realizing she would morph into a fire-breathing dragon. Our identities are powerfully shaped by how we tell our story.

Some stories are all dried up—they have outlived their usefulness. We have told them too many times and squeezed all the juice out of them. Nothing moves inside or out when we tell them. Do you have any stories like these: "*I was foolish to marry so young, I'm a bad father because of, I'm a terrible wife because of?*" What would it be like to gently and gracefully lay these stories down, once and for all? What would it be like to never tell them again?

Other stories still yearn to be told. Old though they may be in time, they still move us. We hear ourselves telling them almost involuntarily. These stories are unfinished business. How can we work with them in ways that lead to healing? How can we transform these stories into ones we *want* to live in?

One method is to choose a story that still contains some pain. Find a good friend and tell the story over and over again. The first time through, most likely you will stir up the many emotions attached to the story. (That's why you work with a good and trusted friend). After telling the story a number of times, you will be able to describe the events much as a video camera would have recorded them. The emotional charge begins to dissipate and you will begin to be able to lay the story to rest.

Gregg Levoy and his wonderful book *Callings* inspires another method of working with challenging events. He wrote, "A tradition in both Middle Eastern and Hebraic mysticism holds that any passage of sacred text, any teaching, any story must be examined from at least three points of view; literal, metaphorical, and universal (mystical or wordless)." (p.47).

I say that each of our human stories is also a sacred story. What would it be like to speak or write your stories from each of these points of view?

For example, assume you recently experienced a big fight with your significant other. First, write or tell the story literally—the "just the facts" version—providing only the phenomena of the events. Describe it as a video camera would have recorded it, leaving aside *all* judgments and editorials. "He didn't respect my opinion" changes into him saying, "What were you thinking?" "She never listens to me" changes into "She rolled her eyes and walked away." Is it challenging to sort out phenomena from conclusions when *we* are one of the main characters? You bet! And this first step, in itself, is potentially very healing.

Tell or write a second version in which you create metaphors for the events that took place. Give yourself room to go overboard, stretching to include symbols, myths, magic and mystery. Incorporate some archetypal characters and themes. (See Appendix A for more images). Purposely embellish the characters, change their motivation, rewrite the plots and create several new endings. Do not be afraid to begin "Once upon a time...."

How does the story unfold if you turn your significant other into a messenger, a demon possessed, or the trickster? What do you learn when you write the story as the loss of paradise, separation from the tribe, a tale of initiation?

The third way would be to write or tell the story fashioning the events as a sacred teaching story. What are the hidden truths waiting to be revealed? Are the events a teaching tale about trust and betrayal, mercy and forgiveness, unconditional love? Tell the story as if you were a wise spiritual teacher teaching your students.

I recently employed these methods while speaking with a patient who lives with the Western medical diagnosis of chronic fatigue syndrome. Extremely busy in her life for a long stretch of time, she was experiencing a profound lack of energy. I asked her, "In mythology, what does the heroine do when tiring from the struggle with the dragon?" She replied, "Time. She has to get away. Go find a cave. Rest. Have time to heal her wounds. Think. Create some distance so she can think what to do next." Any words of mine would have paled in comparison.

Working with personal stories in this way flexes the muscles of your imagination and opens the door to your soul. In healing your story, you expand the personal to embrace the communal and link your particular story with a universal one. Within and beneath the story familiar to you are other versions full of insight and possibilities.

You cannot change the events that have taken place in your past. You can transform the impact of those events into positive influences in your life. Pain is what you bear. The suffering is optional. Why not fashion your life into the most powerful, and compelling story imaginable?

In healing your story, you will heal yourself.

Reflections

Which stories you tell about yourself have run out of juice—nothing moves inside or outside when you tell them? Have they outlived their usefulness? Would it serve to set them aside? Could you do so right now?

Are there some uplifting stories that you tell, ones that others never tire of hearing? Would it serve to write them down as teaching stories for your children, family members, and friends?

Which events do you describe one way to yourself and another way to others? (i.e. why your first husband or wife left…). How might you reconcile these two versions and bring some healing to your self?

If your life were the title of a book, what would that title be? What name would you give to this chapter of your life? What does this reveal about where you are in your life journey?

Practices

You have at least one important life story that still needs to be told, even if no one else ever hears it. This story is the one most in need of healing because it involves so much pain. Write down or record this story and include as many details as you can about how you felt, your thoughts at the time, the impact of the events upon you, etc. Work with the three ways of writing or telling the story as described above. Mark your calendar for one month's time. Read or listen to the versions of the story after that period of time. What has changed by having had an opportunity to tell the story?

As another way of working with a challenging personal story, write about it from a communal point of view. How did the events impact those around you? What do you imagine your partner or spouse, family members, or neighbors would say about the impact of events on them? What do your learn from working with the story in this way?

What are some of your well-worn family stories? What stories bounce around among your group of friends or around the water cooler at work? Are they healing stories? How can you tell them in ways that serve?

4

LIFE AS A UNITY—ONE

When attempting to consider anything in isolation, we find it tied to everything else in the universe.

—John Muir

The ways of being, doing, and speaking outlined thus far can become empty (and ineffective) techniques unless firmly grounded in a philosophical framework. Chapters Four through Eight anchor these distinctions using the symbols of One, Two, Three, Four and Five.

Symbols are signs that suggest something else: something that is larger, not always visible, and yet quite real. Symbols stimulate our imagination and remind us of what we could easily forget. The lion, for example, is often used as a symbol to evoke strength and courage. In the same way, I hope using One, Two, Three, Four, and Five as symbols will offer quick, powerful reminders of important principles.

One symbolizes life as a unity—the deep interrelationship and interconnectedness of all that exists. Because it stands for totality and wholeness, One is the starting and ending point of any conversation about healing.

Two symbolizes life as partnership—the unending dances that show up in the world as "two-ness". Hard *and* soft, fast *and* slow, you *and* I, speaking *and* listening; Two reminds us that life is never just one thing, but rather many things at the same time.

Three symbolizes movement, transformation and change, the magic of life as possibility. Three represents the endlessly fertile and creative field that arises from the coupling of Two.

Four symbolizes the four directions—the North, South, East and West—life expanding to occupy space and time. Four speaks to the critical nature of form, to thoughtfully tend the size and shape of all we create.

Five symbolizes life as nature. In the Chinese wisdom tradition, it is called Wu Hsing—the five movements or phases. Five reminds us of change as the constant in life. We are nature. Each of us contains her endless gifts and can bring them to life through our unique ways of being, doing and speaking.

LIVING THE MYSTERIES

Live the mysteries. Let them infuse your actions and speaking. Remember the words of Rabbi Abraham Heschel, "Just to live is holy. To be is a blessing."

A multitude of shared mysteries bind us together as One, beginning with the improbable fact that we are here at all. We are alive! We are awake! We inhabit bodies! What irreplaceable gifts!

What a boon to receive the wonders of the world through our senses. We can watch the sun rise, hear children play, smell fresh cut grass, taste chocolate, and feel the hot breath of our lover. Above us move an inconceivable sun, an implausible moon, a tapestry of stars, and an ever-changing blue jewel of sky dancing with clouds. Beneath us lies a nourishing, vibrant earth to stand on. We live surrounded by green growing things, a magical, flowing substance called water, and an entire kingdom of animals. We share as well the mysteries of human need and desire, sexuality, love, violence, health, disease, and death.

Returning to consciousness upon rising, all of life appears at the same moment. As we open our eyes we experience the mutual arising and emanations from all that is—the "all at once-ness" of the world. Since ancient times the question has always been asked, "What lies behind it all?" The question expresses our heartfelt desire to give words to the indefinable, unspeakable, and incomprehensible. Science, religion, and philosophy have grown up around the mysteries. Each offers their answers. The ancient ones, however, always knew: that our calculations would always fall short, our beliefs leave us starving, and words on their own would never suffice.

They also knew that we could not leave the question alone. It is a part of our deep human nature to ask, to explore, and to pursue the mystery and meaning of our individual and collective lives.

Reflections

Where in your life do you powerfully experience mysteries?
Which ones intrigue you and won't leave you alone?
What steps do you take to explore them?
How do you respond to the question of the meaning of life?
What do you say is the meaning of *your* life?

Practices

As you move about in the world, take short periods of time to focus on the impressions being received by one sense. For example, focus on what you see—the sources of light, the variety of colors and shadows, how different textures reflect light, etc. Open yourself to awe and appreciation. Record your observations in your practice log. Work separately with each of the senses over the course of a day.

Sometime this week you will lose your observer (i.e. find yourself in reaction) while in the presence of others. When you do so, practice coming back to your senses. Use your senses to reconnect with the present moment. Sit quietly—listen, watch, smell, taste, and feel your body in contact with the world around you.

Do you have a sense of calling or purpose in life? Who is it you are here to become? What is it you are here to do? Can you put answers to these questions into words? Take one week and journal extensively around these questions. Look for recurring themes. See if you can boil down your impressions to one or two sentences and keep your responses where you see them daily.

Mark your calendar. One month after writing about your calling, revisit what you wrote. How is life showing up differently as a result?

BEGIN AND END IN ONE

We are One. It has always been so and will always be so. When we forget, a healing presence calls us back to unity.

Only the rare bird among us has not experienced moments of deep and abiding connection with all that is. Some sense the connection while hearing a piece of beautiful music, others feel it during a hike in the woods, see it in the eyes of a young child, or in those of a dying parent. Any moment can potentially transform into a spiritual occurrence.

Just as exploring the mysteries is part of deep human nature, so too is our pursuit of the transcendent. Truly a mystic lives within us all. We thirst for connection and long for kindred spirits. Quantum physics confirms what mystics of numerous wisdom traditions have known for thousands of years—that relationship is at the heart of the universe. We are deeply interconnected, interdependent, and inseparable from all that is. The Buddhist scholar Thich Nhat Hanh calls this condition inter-being. Here I call it the One, the deep unity of all that is.

For the mass of unenlightened beings (myself surely included), any conscious, embodied experience of Oneness comes and goes. As a phenomenon one *feels* or *experiences*, Oneness appears fleeting and unreliable. I offer Oneness instead as an apriori principle, a declared place from which you choose to live. Oneness can become a stance or posture, a place you call home.

Not being a religion, Oneness requires no faith, no trust, no allegiance, and no belief. It is not an object, a process, or a thing. Oneness exists prior to and behind all distinctions. It is intrinsically impersonal; like the sun that shines or the rain that falls on everyone just the same. Since it embraces everything Oneness is nothing. Since it includes all forms it is formless. Since there is nothing outside of Oneness to measure itself against, it is incomparable.

Try as we like—Oneness is unavoidable. We touch and are touched by, create and are created by everyone and everything around us. Our lives are hopelessly and joyfully embedded in the lives of others and of all living things. We belong to each other.

Oneness is unconditional. It does not depend on you or me, nor does it expect anything of us. There is nothing we can do to damage it. There is nothing to do to "create" Oneness since it has always existed and is already in place.

And, being human, we forget the Oneness and the price of forgetting is high. Fear, isolation, and deadly conflicts have their roots in our forgetting. In the last century alone, some 100 million people died in warfare around the globe. What we can and must do is call each other back, to remind each other when the unity has been forgotten.

Reflections

Can you name one thing you do by yourself? (Eat, sleep, think, die....) Go deeper here. Is there really anything you do by yourself?

Can you name one thing that exists by itself?

Do you create barriers, conditions for Oneness? For example, "when she apologizes then we'll be friends again" or "if he pays me back, then it will be O.K."

What are your assumptions about Oneness—how do you think it should look, sound, and feel? Is Oneness necessarily pleasant or comfortable?

Practices

For a period of time, be attentive to what is spoken around you. When the conversation takes on a tone of "us" vs. "them," ask yourself what you might do to call people back to Oneness. Take a step to do so. Record what happened in your practice log.

At some point this week, you might feel disconnected or isolated from other people or the world around you. When that happens, practice taking a nearby material object and explore how many people were required to bring it present in your life. For example, I am wearing a cotton shirt. I did not plant the cotton, tend it while it was growing, harvest it, clean, dye, weave, or stitch it, box it, truck it, or place it on the store shelf. Dozens of other people whom I will never meet or know did so.

How does your mood change when you think about the world in this way?

LIFE IS NOT BROKEN

All life possesses intrinsic value. Every human life is workable. All healing involves a return—a rediscovering and remembering of unity.

The seamlessness of life reveals another facet of One: life is not broken and there are no missing pieces. Life has integrity, being undivided, complete, and intact just as is. That means *your* life has integrity. You too are whole, unbroken, and missing no pieces. The same can be said for everyone around you.

This moment has integrity, the outcome of every moment that came before (the actual) and the the seed of all that is to come (potential). Ideal, defect, and remedy reside right here, right now. This moment contains all that is needed for life to flourish in the next.

We human beings also forget this facet of the Oneness. We develop amnesia. We believe we are helpless, broken, isolated, somehow separate from the person standing beside us.

To heal we must recover our memory, to once again know what is true, whole and complete. The medieval Christian mystics used the word anamnesis to describe the end of forgetting. Anamnesis is remembering the connection with our many selves, with each other, with all of creation, and with the Divine.

At the heart of healing lies a paradox: that each of us is already whole and complete *and* there is room for transformation and change. Healing occurs when we move:

> *from negative, destructive behaviors* **to** *positive, constructive behaviors*
> *from hurt and wrongdoing* **to** *making things right*
> *from looking back, focusing on the past,* **to** *looking forward, focusing on the future*
> *from fixing blame* **to** *addressing needs and concerns*
> *from denial and remorse* **to** *repentance and forgiveness*
> *from not having a voice* **to** *having a say*
> *from lack of communication* **to** *conversation, dialogue*
> *from a sense of betrayal* **to** *a sense of trust*
> *from isolation, alienation* **to** *connection, collaboration*
> *from being incomplete* **to** *bringing closure*
> *from a lack of empathy* **to** *understanding and respect*
> *from lying and finger pointing* **to** *truth-telling and acknowledgement*
> *from lack of self-worth, meaninglessness* **to** *self-worth and meaning*

*from an imbalance of power, being disempowered **to** restoring equity, being empowered*
*from retribution and punishment **to** reconciliation and restoration*

A healing presence creates a future of less suffering through skillful, heartfelt ways of being, doing, and speaking. The remembering of wholeness can be brought about through touch, a thoughtful word, an acknowledgement, stillness, and even silence. The possibilities are endless. Whatever response we choose in the moment, implicitly we declare that all is One, no matter what. In doing so, we stand on sacred ground.

Reflections

In what ways do you consider yourself whole in body, mind and spirit? In what ways have you considered yourself less than whole? Marred?

How would treating everyone as being whole and complete affect the ways you relate to others?

In what situations do you forget the unity of life?

How do you call yourself back when you've forgotten?

Who do you exclude from your life, believing them to be different from or separate from who you are?

Practices

During the next week you will surely find yourself in a conversation where other individuals or groups are blamed for something, or spoken of as *other than* those present. Find a way to call people back to the unity.

Take one distinct step towards healing and wholeness this week. Choose one movement from the list above and apply it to your life. For example, moving from lack of communication **to** conversation, dialogue: take a step to open (or reopen) the lines of communication with someone in your life. Send an e-mail, write a letter, place a phone call, invite that person to lunch, and so on. Observe what arises in you as you take the step and how life shows up in response. Record your observations in your practice log.

FOR THE SAKE OF...

Whatever you do (or do not do), the actions you take affect the lives of others.
For the sake of all that you care about, accept the call to serve life. You can
do more than you think.

I grew up in a house with three bedrooms and seven family members. My late parents, Bernie and Ruth, slept on a foldout couch in the living room for years and used makeshift closets in the den so their five children could enjoy the bedrooms upstairs. They kept a modest home, did not buy fancy clothes, and never traveled to exotic places. By conserving their resources all five children were able to go to college, an opportunity neither of them had for themselves. Not every moment of their marriage was filled with joy and bliss, yet they never abandoned their posts or complained about their roles. Neither would be considered a saint or martyr. Nevertheless, their quiet heroics demonstrate that contributing to the lives of others is an essential component of a meaningful life.

The phrase *for the sake of* has roots in the Greek "telos", *that for the sake of which*, the goal or outcome, that for which we take an action. Telos is the something or somebody beyond ourselves that gets us moving, a cause or person we yearn to help in order to make a contribution to our shared life. Telos reminds us that nothing in the universe exists just for the sake of itself.

The phrase *for the sake of* can be used to call us back to the shared tasks of ordinary life. It provokes questions that call us back to Large Mind like "What is the larger task here?" or "What is really important?" Individual differences and conflicts tend to melt away in the home, the workplace, and the community when we call ourselves back to the larger task at hand.

Contributing to our shared life looms larger than a good idea or the right thing to do. In serving others, an innate human need is fulfilled. How else to explain what it is that moves us to sacrifice, take risks, extend ourselves, put ourselves out, speak up when it is uncomfortable to do so? We step up to the plate because other living creatures are involved. Our actions serve the lives of those around us.

My patients remind me of what gets them out of bed in the morning. A single mother rises up to take charge of rearing the young ones by herself. A young father contributes two days a week at his child's school. A wealthy matron volunteers at a detox center. An attorney donates her time to a mediation/conflict resolution center.

Crises provide more dramatic examples of this call to action. Without hesitation, we give blood in an emergency, build the levees, and fill a grieving family's house with food. *For the sake of* calls us to partnership beyond the present. It is essential when making social, corporate, or public policy to keep telos in mind, to ask ourselves whether the world we are creating is one in which our children, grandchildren, and great-grandchildren will thrive.

Reflections

Who or what do you live *for the sake of*—your partner, a better life for your children, for God, for freedom?

When you forget, how can you call yourself back to the larger picture? How can you remember that which is really important?

Practices

Take time for reflection. Write down the names of all those who benefit from your being in the world and from what you do in the world. Write down the names of as many family members, friends, co-workers, neighbors, customers, clients, and patients, as you can. Does the length of the list surprise you? Keep the list in a place where you can see it. How does this list affect you?

This same practice is also very powerful in a work setting. Have each member of the group or department where you work write down the names of those who benefit from your collective efforts. Find creative ways to keep this list alive in the members of the group. How does life show up differently when all are aware of how much their work matters?

Take a question such as "What is this for the sake of?" "What is the task?" "What is really important here?" and write it down on a 3x5 card. Carry the card with you for a week. Look at it as you make decisions during your workdays, especially if you become engaged in a conflict or misunderstanding. What effect does the question have on your priorities?

DEATH CALLS TO US

Death is a wake-up call to the preciousness of this moment. Live knowing that you will and must die.

In his Academy Award winning movie *Unforgiven*, Clint Eastwood plays a retired gunslinger coaxed back into the profession to kill a group of outlaws who have disfigured a prostitute. A young braggart joins him along with a character played by Morgan Freeman. The young man shoots the first of the outlaws as he sits in an outhouse. After a narrow escape, the kid starts slugging down whiskey, and it becomes clear he had not killed a man before this day. Bawling through his tears and looking for justification, he turns to Eastwood and says, "I guess he had it coming." Clint looks at him and responds in his classic deadpan voice, "We all have it coming, kid."

And so we do. Woven into the fabric that binds us as One is the truth of our impermanence. We share the same fate as the sun and the moon, the earth and the stars. Sooner or later, quickly or over decades, we lose everything in this world.

Growth, integration, and healing occur as we move through the smaller deaths of our carefully crafted self-images, of our friendships, marriages, dreams, and capacities. Death with a capital "D" holds reign as the ultimate teacher. Nothing shocks us more deeply or sobers us up more quickly. A single glimpse of death turns our world upside down. "My child shouldn't have died before me." "He's ready to die, but I'm not ready for him to die." "I just didn't lose my mother, I lost my best friend." "He was the first person my age that passed away."

Paradoxically, the times of dying and death can also be times of healing. My father was bedridden over the last weeks of his life and during that time my siblings and I shared more physical touch with him than in many years previous. He allowed us to massage his arms, hands, legs, feet, shoulders, and neck. After decades of giving, he was now able to receive. In his last moments, I expected to feel empty and drained. Yet I felt surprisingly full. The harvest had come in. As he had served us, my siblings and I had now served him. The circle between us was complete.

Our yesterdays no longer exist. Our tomorrows are never guaranteed. How exquisite, the pain and joy of realizing this moment is all we have.

Reflections

What are some of the smaller deaths you have experienced in your life—self-image, friendships, skills and abilities, etc.?

How have you responded to each one?

In what ways have the physical deaths of others already shaped your life?

How does the knowledge of your own death impact how you are, what you do, and what you say?

Practices

Practice carrying with you a small reminder of your own death, even if it is only a card with the words "I Will Die" on it. How does this increased awareness affect your choices and decisions during this time?

We never know when the people around us or ourselves will die. Is there something that really needs to be spoken to a family member, friend, relative, or co-worker? Do not delay. Have one of those conversations. Write that letter. Make sure the words get spoken.

Take time to reflect. If you were to die this week, would the life you have lived express your core values? Are you responding to your calling? Fulfilling your purpose? What steps might you take to bring your life even more into alignment with your values? Record your notes in your practice log.

A CHALLENGE

Accept the limitations posed by language. Maintain the One within a language that reinforces duality and separation. Keep the world in one piece.

When you were learning the English language, do you remember the process of diagraming sentences on the board? It seemed like all of life had to be either a noun or a verb. Subjects acted upon objects. The singular flow of time was chopped into the past, present or future. The words *you* and *me* implied something quite different, the words *them* and *us* lived worlds apart. All on their own, words can leave us with the impression of a separated, disjointed, oppositional world.

Language completes what the senses begin. Through it, we create distinctions and give names to the infinite phenomena of the world. We name our *percep*-tions: red, wet, sweet, loud, and sharp. We name our *con*ceptions: justice, racism, and peace. Language shapes not only how we look at the world, it directs what we see in the world.

Making distinctions is essential for survival: I do want to know the difference in meaning between "Watch out for that car" and "Have a nice day." We run a big risk, however, in tugging apart the world into separate names. At the end of the day, we may forget to put the world back together again.

Every being, structure, object, process, and event is always *more than* any single name or label we might use to describe it:

> Patients are *more than* their disease.
> Elderly are *more than* their ages.
> Convicts are *more than* their crime.
> Computers are *more than* a tool.
> Marriage is *more than* an institution.
> Sports are *more than* a distraction.
> September 11th is *more than* a tragedy.

Forgetting the *more than* is another form of amnesia, one more way we create unnecessary suffering. A healing presence cultivates the skill of putting the world back together again and calls us back to the richness of life.

Reflections

What aspects of your work and life require that you compare/contrast, analyze, dissect, diagnose? How do these processes affect how you view the world?

How do you call yourself back to the Oneness in the presence of these tasks?

Practices

Pay close attention to how people use language. Note the percentage of time language is used to dissect and break apart the world compared to how often it is used to express the interconnectedness of life. What did you hear? How does this exercise affect how you use your words? Write down your findings in your practice log.

Choose a period of time in which to consciously use your words to express the interconnectedness of all that appears around you. What do you notice? How did the conversation change?

5

LIFE AS A DANCE—TWO

....Indeed, the hidden and the manifest give birth to each other.
Difficult and easy complement each other.
Long and short exhibit each other.
High and low set measure to each other.
Voice and sound harmonize each other.
Back and front follow each other. .

—Lao Tze
Tao Teh Ching, No. 2
Wu translation

Two is another way to speak of the One. It reflects the quality of "two-ness" in the world—the knowing of singular aspects of life through relationship. For example, it is a challenge to understand what is meant by the word hot unless we have a sense of cold, difficult to grasp wet unless there is dry, hard to conceive of heaven without knowing hell. Aspects of the Two are inseparable from each other. You know this if you have ever been speaking and realized no one was listening, or were attempting to lead and no one was following.

Two is the One expressing itself as movement, the lively dance back and forth between different states of being and doing. In the *Way of Heaven* (p.14), Pere Larre wrote, "For the world to be alive, it must beat. 2 is the beating." This morning I noticed I was quite active, this afternoon I am resting. At times I am playful, at other times serious. I tend to be quiet and at times can be quite loud.

Two symbolizes the intrinsic partnerships in the natural world and in the domain of human activity. It speaks to mutual arising: multiple phenomena occurring in the world simultaneously. As life unfolds the world expands from one possibility to this and this and this. Two allows us to hold life not as a singular thing, but as many things at the same time.

Two calls us back to the unity by focusing our attention on the relationship between things rather than the things themselves. Two reminds us we are connected to everyone and everything in the universe in the eternal dance of energy.

MUTUAL ARISING

*Acknowledge that you are a human paradox—both this **and** that. By embracing your dual nature, you become a living expression of the One.*

One day while returning home from a walk I noticed a car in the parking lot which had every seat filled to the windows with books, clothing, boxes, old newspapers and grocery bags, you know—stuff! I immediately jumped into Small Mind, creating stories of how messy this person must be, what chaos their life must be in, how lazy they are, etc. Suddenly—a small epiphany—I realized there were areas of my own life that were messy and chaotic, areas in which I keep around piles of stuff. In pointing to the other, I realized I was also pointing to myself.

Nature provides a living model of the dual nature of life. As you read the list of qualities and processes below, note how each aspect is intrinsically connected to and defined by its partner.

hot/cold	wet/dry	hard/soft
light/dark	rising/falling	sound/silence
young/old	growth/decay	fast/slow
weak/strong	calm/storm	peaks/valleys
stillness/movement	night/day	clear/cloudy
earth/sky	deep/shallow	flexible/rigid
living/dying	creation/destruction	heaven/earth

Another way to picture these relationships is to imagine the arc created by the movement of a pendulum. The dance of life moves back and forth along the arc in the human landscape as well as in nature. For example, I begin most days in meditation. I am comfortable one moment and uncomfortable in the next. Now my mind is focused, in the next moment it wanders. My attention moves inward to an ache in my leg, and then is drawn outward to the sound of sparrows outside my window.

I observe a similar movement throughout the day. I am thoughtful with a patient in the treatment room and then thoughtless to another driver on the road, articulate in a conversation with a colleague and then fumbling for words in the classroom, attentive to getting my exercise and then not paying attention to my choice for dinner.

Below is a list of interesting and sometimes surprising partners in the domain of human activity. As you read the examples, picture the partners as end points of a pendulum's arc. How do you move back and forth along these continuums?

listening/speaking	leading/following	being/doing
giving/receiving	opening/closing	pleasure/pain
taking in/letting go	certain/uncertain	cooperation/opposition
balance/imbalance	absolute/relative	hidden/manifest
conscious/unconscious	acceptance/denial	health/disease
teaching/learning	success/failure	personal/communal
thinking/feeling	playful/serious	rational/intuitive
left brain/right brain	reveal/conceal	contraction/expansion
sacred/secular	beginner/master	internal/external
unify/divide	stopping/going	simple/complex
pure/tainted	small mind/large mind	peace/war
innocent/worldly	direct/indirect	difficult/easy
competent/incompetent	spontaneous/planned	forbid/allow
energy/structure	remember/forget	positive/negative
quiet/loud	seeking/bringing	attraction/aversion
creation/destruction	clarity/confusion	mythos/logos
dependent/independent	strange/familiar	limited/unlimited
appropriate/inappropriate	literal/metaphorical	

Do you find that with some pairs you tend to reside on one end of the arc? Do you disapprove or have judgments about one side of the coin, say *opposition* or *disease*, as compared to their partners, *cooperation* and *health*? Do you find that in some domains you were well practiced at, or a master at one side (leading, teaching, or speaking) and more of a beginner at the other (following, learning, or listening)? Several practices at the end of the chapter will help you recalibrate yourself, so you can experience more ease in moving back and forth along the arc.

When in Small Mind, you forget the Oneness, that you are a *both/and* phenomenon containing both sides of the coin within your being. In forgetting, you divide yourself and the world, approving or desiring only one side of the coin, disapproving or rejecting the other. The predictable outcomes are internal or external conflict and unnecessary suffering.

In Large Mind, you acknowledge both sides of the coin as true, inseparable complements and recognize that you move back and forth between them all the time. Some days you are at war, other days at peace. Some days you are moving towards health, other days moving toward disease. Today your heart is open; tomorrow it may be closed.

As you grow stronger in being a healing presence, you will increasingly come to know your tendencies. In acknowledging your own tendencies, you will become more tolerant, understanding, and forgiving of yourself and others.

Reflections

In the pairs that reflect the human landscape, did you find yourself strongly disapproving or rejecting one side of the coin? Can you begin to see where the other side also shows up in you?

In which pairs did you see yourself more practiced in, or a master of one side, and a beginner at the other? How might you gain more practice integrating the other side?

Practices

During the next week, when you observe yourself judging another person, give a name to the "negative" qualities you see—arrogance, stinginess, disrespect, etc. Write down in your practice log some examples of where in *your* life that same quality shows up. For example, I am arrogant about x, I am stingy with y, I am disrespectful towards z. Does this process soften your judgments towards others?

Take a period of time to do the same with "positive" traits that you observe; those you admire in others, yet feel you do not possess. For example, if you observe a person being really thoughtful to another, write down where and how *you* are thoughtful. Does this process reveal some hidden qualities that you were unaware of in yourself?

Take a step this week to recalibrate yourself along a given arc. If you are finding life too complex, for example, take steps to simplify it. Let go of that class you were going to take, or put down the book you lost interest in two weeks ago. If life is too simple, add complexity (and aliveness) by throwing a big party for no reason, or volunteering some of your time for the next few months. Write about how these actions shifted how you move along the arc.

THE BEAUTY OF *AND*

Living in a black or white world, an either/or world creates surplus suffering. Choose to live in a both/and world, one that is rich, complex, and filled with possibility.

While I don't remember the exact moment, I do know there came a time while treating patients when I realized how powerfully my worldview had been affected by Western reductionism. In my attempts to have patients be specific about the phenomena that were taking place in their bodies, I spoke in polarities: "Is it a dull ache or is it sharp?" "Did this come on gradually or all of a sudden?" "Is it better or worse with exercise?"

I learned from my patients that life doesn't reduce to opposites—life shows up as many things at the same time. They would respond, "Mostly I have a dull pain and sometimes it's really sharp." "My back gradually started hurting a week ago and last night I couldn't even bend over." "My headaches are better when I go swimming and worse when I play volleyball." So much for being specific! My questions were subtle attempts to flatten complexities and simplify phenomena that were anything but simple.

Over time I noticed how pervasive *either/or* had become in daily usage. Fortunately, the word *and* shines as a bright light within our language. When substituted for the words *but* and *or,* the word *and* reminds us of the complexity of life and acts as an antidote to duality. It balances our tendency to separate and isolate the phenomena of life. The word *and* helps us to maintain the Oneness despite a language prone to dissection.

As a healing word *and:*

Binds together polarities, ambiguities and contradictions

*I am committed to this relationship **and** I am not sure I trust you right now.*
*I love the people I work with **and** I hate my job.*
*I'm excited about our vacation **and** I don't want to stay the full week.*

Makes room for two phenomena to go on simultaneously

*I'm glad you told me **and** I'm angry that you waited so long.*
*I'm happy you're getting married **and** I'll miss having you as a roommate.*
*I respect your opinion **and** I'm afraid you're making the wrong decision.*

Allows for greater possibilities

*Let's include the managers **and** the staff in the next meeting.*
*We'll go to dinner first **and** take in the movie afterwards.*
*Let's help Susan move this morning **and** go for a walk in the afternoon.*

You may have noticed in the first two categories how the word *and* showed up where you normally expect to see the word *but*. That was deliberate. As a practice, I avoid the word. The word *but* tends to discount everything spoken before it, as if the part after the word *but* were the only important part of the communication. The word *but* pits two phenomena against each other and slows down the forward movement of expression. When you substitute the word *and* for *but*, life became more spacious and workable.

Reflections

What are some of the polarities and contradictions you identify as "difficult" in your life? (e.g. I need to lose weight, *but* I hate to exercise.) What happens in your body when you use the word *and* to connect the two?

Do you have mixed feelings about someone or something in your life? How is it different when you use the word *and* to acknowledge and connect these feelings?

Practices

Make it your practice to listen for the word *but* in conversations. What do you observe when it is used? Write down the observations in your practice log.

For a day, consciously substitute the word *and*, used as in the examples above. How does life show up differently around you?

When you realize you are in *either/or* conversations, find ways to expand into more than two possibilities. Could your options include this and this and this?

DECLARING PARTNERSHIP

Relationship lies at the heart of healing. Declare your partnership with all of life. Remember that which joins us together.

For a period of time my colleague, John Sullivan, had a wonderful practice upon rising. Each morning he would have a dialogue with the mirror in his bathroom that would go something like this:

> *Mirror: John?*
> *John: Yes.*
> *Mirror: Are you awake?*
> *John: Yes I am.*
> *Mirror: Practice partnership.*
> *John: I will.*

What would it be like to begin every morning declaring your partnership with everyone and everything around you—no matter what? What if your declared partners included the young one who is running late for school again, the gas station attendant who never meets your eyes, the co-worker still fuming over a remark you made last week?

The most difficult challenge in the dance of Two is holding self and other together as One. Our notion of *self* usually includes a "something" residing inside our skin, and *other* as "something" encapsulated inside another skin. In addition to these tenuous notions, our forays into Small Mind offer another challenge. Self and other are not held as two sides of a single coin, they deteriorate into opposition, self versus other, us versus them.

Opposition has some short-lived benefits—we feel good and righteous, and a good scrape often energizes us. Life seen as continuous battle can be very seductive until we learn how to convert those struggles into a dance. In fact, that is one way to shift your internal stance—by asking yourself the question, "How can I dance with this?"

Learning to dance with others takes more than a few lessons. Each person is different; therefore each dance is different. Be the other a spouse, family member, friend, or co-worker, partnering them with skill must be an ongoing practice. Discovering the knack of "getting along" goes on for a lifetime.

As with all facets of life, partnerships shift and change over time. A husband and wife face each other over breakfast one morning, only to realize their children have grown and left home. A good friend of yours gets married and has less time for shared interests. The company you work for gets reorganized and your new job description lacks excitement. Disappointment and opposition begin to bubble up from the depths.

Defining (and redefining) the purpose of our shared lives is as important as articulating the meaning of our individual lives. Husband and wife now have an opportunity to redefine their marriage. Two good friends can take steps to find quality time together. The company reorganization offers you the possibility of reexamining work and career. The steps of the dance are created anew.

Reflections

Where in your life do you assume the stance of *me vs. you, us vs. them*? What would being in partnership look like, sound like, and feel like?

Where in your life have you forgotten the purpose of a partnership—with your spouse/partner, family members, friends? How might you recreate or redefine the purpose of your being together?

Practices

Work with a personal relationship in your life where you experience a lack of partnership. What small step would move you toward dancing? Take that step this week.

Have a conversation with a family member, friend, or co-worker. Ask for specific ways that you might become a better partner for that person (i.e. what helps to makes them laugh, how to give them feedback, or what motivates them in moments of discouragement). Adopt their answer as a practice you take on for the sake of the relationship.

6

LIFE AS POSSIBILITY—THREE

Creation is only the projection into form of that which already exists.

—Srimad Bhagavatam

Three is yet another way to express the ever-changing One. It symbolizes the magic of creation—the energy that connects and unites Two, thus bringing about new life. Think of the trinities of Heaven, Earth, and Human, Father, Son, and Holy Ghost, mother, father, and child. Think of the marriage of past with present to create the future. Three symbolizes movement, transformation, and change. It stands for the dynamic equilibrium that is life itself.

Consider how the warmth of the sun's rays meets the cool dawn air and produces a fresh morning breeze. Two teens imitating each other on the dance floor will magically create a new dance between them. In reviewing my teaching notes, a colleague reveals new possibilities of how I can present my class.

Three can be likened to an endlessly fertile and generative field in which different elements come together to create something different than any single force could create alone. In Three, new possibilities come into being, and the world is never again the same.

THE MAGIC OF THREE

Every moment is an act of creation. Use your power to bring visions and dreams into existence.

Picture the writer staring at her blank page, the artist glaring at his empty canvas, a gardener facing a tangle of weeds. A mysterious "something" begins to stir between the two. In the next moment, the hand is scribbling, the paintbrush flying, the hoe tearing away at the earth. In a single moment of creation a door opens to imagination and soul. Anything is possible.

> *....One gave birth to Two*
> *Two gave birth to Three*
> *Three gave birth to all the myriad things.*

> Lao Tze
> Tao Teh Ching No. 42
> *Wu translation*

The myriad things Lao Tze points to are also called the ten thousand things, a Chinese metaphor for everything that exists between heaven and earth. Ten thousand is considered too many to count—hence infinity. The infinite expressions of life include ten thousand breaths and heartbeats, days and nights, desires and disappointments, joys and sorrows, loves and losses, births and deaths. Ten thousand possibilities—the image beautifully captures the ongoing nature of creation, the capacity of life to keep on making new life again and again and again.

> *There are ten thousand ways to:*
> *be*
> *do*
> *speak*
> *feel*
> *think*
> *imagine*
> *understand*
> *relate to*
> *respond*
> *express.*
> *Too many to count.*

Life gets turned upside down in the process of creation. Picture the messy writing table during the first draft, the chaotic artist's studio and the half-finished painting, the garden littered with torn up weeds. Out of chaos comes the new creation.

Is part of your life in chaos? Good! It may be a sign that life is on the move. Something new is seeking to be born.

Reflections

In recalling the times when you were highly creative, what do you find to be the essential ingredients of creativity for you?

Are they presently in place in your life?

What are you creating together in your relationships with family members, friends, and colleagues?

Practices

Take a creative endeavor you are involved in and speak about it with a friend. Ask them for their constructive thoughts, impressions, and feelings about the project. How does this conversation expand your sense of what is possible? Write down these impressions in your practice log.

Working with a close friend or partner, describe a place in your life that is "stuck" (a friendship that has soured, a logjam at work, etc.) Turn the situation upside down; twist it around; look at it fresh. Create at least three stories of how you could create some movement. In addition to being practical and rational, be silly, funny, irrational, and implausible.

Choose one of the possibilities and act on it. Take on the practice of creating three stories of how you might proceed in any situation.

TENDING THE RICE POT

Movement, transformation, and change are taking place all around you.
Take the simple steps that keep life moving forward.

The Chinese character for chi has been loosely translated as breath, life force, vitality, and energy. The ideogram depicts the vapors or steam rising from cooking rice, moving the lid of the pot up and down. The rice is not just sitting on the shelf; it is cooking—on its way to becoming nourishment. The character portrays movement as synonymous with life, transformation and change as ongoing realities.

A healing presence takes the necessary steps to keep the lid on the rice pot bubbling smoothly up and down. He (or she) supplies the necessary fuel, adds more water, and adjusts the heat as needed. No heat—nothing happens. Not enough heat, the lid stills. Too much heat and the whole thing might blow!

The vapors from the bubbling rice pot also reveal a change of substance taking place inside. Inedible rice transforms into nourishment for all. The process hints of alchemical changes and will be explored in depth later in this chapter.

Life calls us to tend many different rice pots. Our families, friendships, communities, corporations, states, countries, and world need tending on a regular basis. As a mother we apply the Band-Aid to our child's scraped knee and kiss the pain away. As a spouse or partner we provide encouragement and support. At work, we tend to an upset co-worker who is down in the dumps. Maybe the neighborhood needs some willing bodies to clean up the empty lot. A healing presence creates the conditions in which the whole tribe flourishes.

More specific forms of tending will be discussed as you proceed through the book. For now, please focus on the simple fact: life is movement. Tending the rice pot often consists of basic steps that keep life moving—getting out of bed, seeing the children off to school, initiating the phone call, writing the condolence card.

Little steps create big changes over time. My T'ai Chi Ch'uan teacher, Ben Lo, compared the practice of t'ai chi ch'uan and the discipline of writing. One round of practice each day is like writing one page each day. Over the course of a year the effects of daily practice add up—and as far as writing goes—you would have a book!

Let the world take care of itself for a while. Forward the movement of life that is taking place in front of you right here, right now. Take on the practice of holding simple questions. What is needed here? What will allow life to flourish in this place, in this moment? How can I create healthy movement?

Reflections

In what domains are you directly responsible for tending the rice pot? (Aspects of family life, distinct responsibilities at work, caring for an ailing friend). Are all the ingredients in place and present in the right proportion? What else do you need to tend the pot?

When your own life gets stuck, like the lid on the rice pot, what ways have you discovered to get it moving again?

What strategies do you employ when disappointed or discouraged with your efforts to tend?

Practices

In the next social event you attend, watch how all the different ingredients (people, food, music, conversation, activities) come together. Without any great fanfare, help the host or hostess tend the pot. When something needs doing; do it. Simply assist in keeping life moving—creating the conditions in which the party will flourish. Afterwards, reflect on what you learned, including your own degree of enjoyment. Describe the experience in your practice log.

Choose a specific area in the work place where you observe that life is not moving smoothly. What will it take to get the lid on the rice pot smoothly bubbling up and down? Having a conversation with the boss? Offering acknowledgements at a staff meeting? Celebrating someone's birthday? Take steps to get life moving again.

Where are you a beginner at tending a particular rice pot? Are you a new mom or dad? Have you recently taken charge of the youth group at your church or been given new responsibilities at work? Who can help you with your tending? What resources are close by that you could call on to assist you? Gather the resources you need this week.

TAKING RISKS: PARADOX AND PROVOCATION

Provoke. Perturb. Disturb. Challenge. Push back. Take risks in the service of life.

No one would deny that our individual and collective lives become stagnant. All too often we find ourselves digging deeper and deeper ruts or spinning in endless circles. At times like these, it helps to disturb the personal and collective paradigms that are in place. At times like these, we need to vigorously stir the pot!

I am not urging you to create movement just for movement's sake and hope for the best. More often than not, these erratic actions only cause more suffering. I am speaking about the challenge of creating healthy movement that calls us to wholeness.

Think of some modern historical figures that profoundly disturbed life—Gandhi who would not eat, Martin Luther King who marched, Rosa Parks who simply said no. Their actions were direct, purposeful, and disturbing.

Two effective ways to stir the pot are paradox and provocation.

Paradox

Many times over the years I have found myself in the treatment room with patients who, for whatever reasons, did not talk much. At first, in an effort to engage them, I would speed up my conversation and ask even more questions. Over time, however, I learned that these methods seldom work. Now I greet silence by sitting still, speaking slowly and less often. As a result, patients frequently begin to speak more freely about themselves.

The story exemplifies how paradox can be used to stir up the pot. In many situations, *stillness creates movement* and *silence provokes speaking.*

On occasion, going against your habits and intuitions will stir the pot. If nothing else, you will get a fresh look at what is happening. The phrase counter-intuitive may be the modern synonym for a paradoxical response.

Thirty years ago while doing programs with the Arica Institute, I adopted the idea of creating a morning routine. To this day, I devote the first 45-60 minutes of the day to self-care. The routine may included anything from meditation, chanting, a round of T'ai Chi Ch'uan, or even a short jog. I inevitably leave home feeling awake, alert, and ready for the day. This structured time frees me up to fully tend others. Incorporating this routine is an example of *structure creating freedom.*

Can you think of other examples? A time when you found light in the darkness? Or discovered courage and strength in the midst of illness? Had moments of joy while suffering?

Provocation

Thirty years ago I took a college course in twentieth-century American literature from a professor named Arthur Gitlen. My fellow students and I were predominantly from small towns in upstate New York. That is, we were young **and** naive. On the reading list was Hubert Selby's *Last Exit to Brooklyn*, a searing portrayal of disintegrating human lives.

I will never forget how Professor Gitlen began his discussion of the book.

"You students make me laugh. You think you go out to the bars on the weekends looking for *love*, looking for *the one*…. I'll tell you why you really go to the bars. It's real simple. YOU'VE GOT AN ITCH AND YOU WANT SOMEONE TO SCRATCH IT."

Thirty jaws dropped to the floor and the room exploded in response, "What are you talking about?" "No way." "That's not true." "We're not like those people in the book." For the next two hours we sat on the edge of our seats in a heated conversation about love, sexuality, aggression, and violence in the early 70's.

Gitlen was provocative. He took a risk in order to serve our learning. He perturbed the cherished images we had of ourselves and challenged us to take a closer look at our lives. On that morning, he was a powerful healing presence.

Is it risky to go against your own habitual ways, to purposely rock the boat? You bet. Might these methods also create more suffering? At times they do. And, we need to ask, what is the cost of *not* disturbing life in this manner?

I learned in the treatment room over the years that we are not as fragile as we might think. People invariably grow and change in response to adversity and challenge. Go ahead. Push back. Hard truths save lives.

Reflections

In recalling the people who have had a profound influence on your life, did some provoke and disturb you?

Did they take a risk? Challenge you? Push back against you?

What aspects of your personal life would benefit from being perturbed right now?

Practices

Create a dinner for your partner, spouse or family. Speak little while serving the food. Continue to eat in friendly silence. Observe how others respond.

Write an entry in your practice log about a "predicament" in which you currently find yourself. Exaggerate all the morbid details until your story gets ridiculous. Blow up the problem until it becomes so huge—even Superman couldn't solve it! What, of substance, now reveals itself?

Practice taking an aspect of your life with others that has become stagnant or predictable and consciously disturb it. Do something different. If you always get together with a friend for lunch, go for a walk instead. Go to a play or a movie. Bring along a third party. Stir the pot!

Take a plan you have for the future (i.e. meeting with your boss, taking a trip with a friend) and take a risk. Purposefully insert an unknown into the event. How did making this change affect how the event unfolded?

TURNING LEAD INTO GOLD

Act as a humble assistant in the process of transformation. Create the conditions for turning lead into gold.

Do you remember the images of the alchemists from the Middle Ages, feverishly working on formulas that would transform base metals into gold? In the literal sense, they failed. Their efforts were in vain. When we view their work as metaphor, however, their work points us to an essential component of healing: we can transform the substance of our lives.

Each of us possesses portions of lead. Painful circumstances and events are common ingredients in all human lives. Perhaps a parent died while we were young. Perhaps we had an alcoholic father or an unfaithful spouse. Perhaps we have developed a chronic medical condition. Or worse, perhaps one of our children did, and died as a result.

Such events are quite real and cannot be made to disappear. We can, however, transform our relationship to them.

Just as in the alchemical formulas, our personal transformation requires a catalyst and the components of heat, pressure and time. Desire acts as the catalyst. Our heat is the warmth of love and mercy (for ourselves as well as the others involved). Awareness and attention provide the pressure. Stir in the gift of time and our formula for transformation is complete.

On the same day that I completed the first draft of this chapter, the American cyclist Lance Armstrong completed his third inspiring win of the Tour de France—this, five years into his struggle with metastasized testicular cancer. (Since then he has won two more.) His accomplishment provides an extraordinary example of transforming suffering into offering.

Other less dramatic and more private examples surround us in abundance. You probably know several such people: the alcoholic or addict who gets clean and counsels those still in the grips, those living with AIDS who speak to students about unprotected sex, or the students with learning disabilities who go on to become scholars. Every day such journeys through the dark night of the soul are transformed into life-changing lessons and powerful teaching stories for the rest of us.

The alchemical cooking of lead into gold does not happen overnight, nor is it altogether pleasant. Often we are unable to see how our struggles might be perceived as gifts and we despair that anything of value will come from them. At times, the journey may seem to leave us stranded in darkness and pain.

What matters is that we keep stirring the pot—that we keep moving forward with whatever pain and effort are required.

Below are some ways we can convert our lead into gold. We can transform:

Suffering into offering
Obstacles, challenges into opportunities
Wounds, illnesses into gifts
Conflicts into possibilities
Weaknesses into strengths
Nemeses into allies
Complaints into requests
No into Yes

Reflections

Is there anyone who entered your life as a nemesis and is now an ally (family member, classmate, friend, co-worker)? How did that transformation take place?

What in your life do you label a problem? Have you been willing to experience the situation fully or have you been avoiding some aspect of it? Are you resisting "cooking" the lead into gold?

What else is possible with that situation? How might you transform it into an opportunity—for better communication, perhaps? Is it an opportunity to let go or listen more closely?

Practices

Take a situation in your present life involving others that you would simply like to go away. Working with the catalyst of desire, the warmth of love and mercy, the pressure of awareness and the gift of time, how might you transform the situation? Begin taking those steps this week.

Document the journey in your practice log.

Choose a past event or period in your life in which you experienced pain and suffering. How could you now change that suffering into an offering? Would it serve to write about it, volunteer or work with others who are going through the same process? How will you complete the transformation of lead into gold?

7

LIFE IN THE FOUR DIRECTIONS—FOUR

Form follows function.

—Frank Lloyd Wright

Energy accumulates. Any creation coming into being expands to occupy time and space. If the Three speaks to life as movement, transformation, and change, Four symbolizes the methods we use to assess movement and change within time and space.

The four directions of the compass (North, South, East, West) symbolize the structures we create to organize and orient ourselves to nature and reality. Similar, essential constructs that come in fours include the basic operations of arithmetic (addition, subtraction, multiplication, division), the basic geometric shapes (line, circle, triangle, square), and the four seasons (spring, summer, fall, winter).

Try to imagine functioning in a world without the constructs described above—a world without math, science, architecture, alphabets, clocks, calendars, maps, currency, charts and graphs of all kinds. Quite a formula for chaos! The Four provides us with ways to order and sequence the infinite activity of the One.

How does the Four relate to being a powerful healing presence? Four speaks to the critical nature of design: consciously crafting how your good intentions will be translated into form.

For example, say you would like to acknowledge a co-worker for the help they have given you at work. The form of the acknowledgement consists of the who, what, when, where, and how. Who will be involved? What will you say? Where and when will you deliver the acknowledgement? How will you deliver the acknowledgement (via a lunch, a letter, a gift)?

Consciously designing your offerings with the recipient in mind greatly increases the likelihood they will be received by others. Healing comes about by design rather than coincidence.

Taking Effective Action

Our communications and interactions with others are a distinct form of cre-
ation. Consciously designing your offerings makes it more likely that others
will receive your care and compassion.

Taking effective action in the world revolves around communication. Whether you are making requests, offering feedback, providing explanations, sharing opinions, or delivering acknowledgements, the design of your communication makes a difference.

One way to think through your offering to another is to ask yourself the classic journalist's questions: Who? What? When? Where? How? For example, say you want to have an important conversation with your teenager about some behavior that is of concern. The format below offers one way to think through the process ahead of time. By doing so, you increase the likelihood that your actions will be well received.

Who?

There are several aspects to consider. Who is this for the sake of? Name those who will benefit from this conversation (your teenager, other siblings, you, your spouse). Who will be in the room when you have the conversation? Will it serve to have your spouse/partner or other siblings present or not? Can you use input from others ahead of time?

What?

Write down your intentions beforehand. What do you want to communicate? What specific outcomes are you looking for? Do you want to create new goals? Set boundaries? Convey concern? Offer comfort? Acknowledge the positive? Reassure?

When?

Timing is important. When would be the best time to have the conversation? Does morning or afternoon make a difference? Is it better to do have the conversation over a quiet meal? Will it serve to have the conversation right away or is it better to wait? Sometimes our observer needs to be more firmly in place before we proceed!

Where?

Where will the conversation take place? Would it help to be indoors, in a contained space? Better to be outdoors while taking a walk? Would meeting in public support the process?

How?

Your actions grow in power when content, voice, posture, gestures, and physical touch are congruent. What will you look like, sound like, and feel like during the conversation? What is the tenor or tone that will serve? How might you use touch to amplify your speaking and intention? Practice beforehand by yourself or with others to improve your delivery.

At first, all these questions may seem *just a bit much!* In learning how to take effective action, you will probably feel self-conscious for a time, doing something consciously that you had not given much thought to before. Even with experience the actions you take may not always produce the outcome you anticipated and that's o.k. Time will determine whether your actions served. Effects may continue to unfold over days, weeks, months, and even years.

At the same time, trust that you will continue to learn and naturally develop a greater sense of what really serves the people around you. As you begin to master design and form you will become more skillful at transforming your care and compassion into effective actions

Reflections

What is the form of your relationship with your boss?
—How often are you in contact with him/her?
—Do you communicate primarily in person, via e-mail, phone calls, in real or virtual time?
—How often are you in the same room at the same time?
—Are others always a part of the conversation?
Would it serve to shift any aspect of the relationship?

What is the form of your most troubled relationship in the personal realm? What changes in form can you make that might get this relationship moving again?

The last time you offered an acknowledgement to someone, would you say it was received? Looking back, what might you have done differently to make it easier for the other to take in?

Practices

Take one or two steps to change the form of the next meeting you are involved in. Alter the configuration of tables or chairs. Consider sitting in a circle instead of at a table. Sit in a different seat than you normally do. Ask others to do the same. Add to the agenda or shift items around. Notice how people respond. How did the changes impact the tone and outcome of the meeting? Anchor your observations in your practice log.

In the next week, use the journalist's questions (who, what, when, where, how) to take effective action with a family member, friend or co-worker. How did the design you chose affect how your offering was received?

Work to design one effective action (what we might call treatment) each week and deliver it to another person, group, or organization in your life. Describe the process and outcomes in your practice log.

SHIFTING PARADIGMS

Paradigms that serve are those that reveal our individual and collective lives to be a unity. They renew our sense of partnership and wholeness. Be aware of the internal and external forms that shape your life. Contribute to the task of healing the social systems and institutions around you.

The story goes that a young man and his wife stopped at a small-town gas station to ask directions. They were considering a move to the area and asked the elderly attendant what the local people were like. The old man asked, "What are people like where you come from?" The young man responded, "Well most of them are pretty cold. They tend to keep to themselves and we find them pretty snobby." The old man replied, "I think you will find people to be the same way here."

Two days later another young couple stopped at the same gas station, and they too asked the old man what people were like in the region. He asked them, "How do you find people to be like where you come from?" The young man responded, "They're terrific! Very friendly and outgoing, really helpful, always eager to lend a hand." The old man replied, "I expect you will find them to be the same way here."

Like these couples, what you expect in life is likely what you will get. Your thoughts, assumptions, beliefs, and conclusions form models and patterns of how the world works. Taken together these internal paradigms shape how you perceive and interpret your experiences.

Maybe you have nodded to a new co-worker and noticed he didn't return your acknowledgement. "Self-absorbed" is one conclusion you could make. "Must be from the East Coast" could be another. "Still getting his feet on the ground" could be a third. Which (if any) interpretation would most likely lead to a connection with this person in the future? Whether we are conscious of our paradigms or not, they impact how life shows up around us.

The paradigms we adopt change over time. For example, in my early teens I operated from a simple paradigm: those in positions of power and authority know what they are doing. I assumed our leaders were well-intentioned, smart, experienced, and exercised good judgment. The political culture of the 50's and early 60's supported that paradigm.

Then came the Vietnam War, which dented my paradigm badly. Years spent working in the private sector then blew it wide open. I began to operate from a very different paradigm: all of us are making it up as we go along.

The good news is you get to choose what you think. The constructs you adopt shape your habits, values, politics, and morals. Jogging three times a week arises from your paradigm of what constitutes good health. Balancing a checkbook reflects your paradigm of what it is to be fiscally responsible. Having your child inoculated with vaccines reflects your paradigm of what it is to be a good parent.

A society's collective paradigms are shaped by influential groups of like-minded people who construct the world in similar ways. For example, in the waning days of 2002 politicians and the multitude of talking heads on network television were constantly speaking of *weapons of mass destruction*. Specifically they meant the means for conducting biological, chemical, and nuclear warfare. Omitted from this paradigm were many other phenomena which some would say fit the same description—*weapons of mass destruction*—cigarettes, alcohol, drugs, automobiles, domestic violence, guns, poverty, or illiteracy.

Collective paradigms need to be examined regularly since over time they solidify into public policy and social systems. For example, out of what assumptions does the phenomenon *high school* come from, and what would our education system look like without it? How did the notion of *prison* come about and does it really serve victims, offenders, and members of the larger community? Where did the notion of *insurance* originate? What are the benefits of these structures? What are the shortcomings? What do we fail to see when we assume each of these systems as a given?

Your challenge as a healing presence is to stay conscious of the personal and collective paradigms from which you operate. Every paradigm reveals and conceals, sheds light and creates shadows, encourages some behaviors and discourages others. There is always more to life than can be expressed through any single paradigm.

The placards of the 60's read, "Challenge authority!" The placards of this new century might well read, "Challenge paradigms!" Questioning and challenging collective paradigms requires perseverance. Looking freshly at shared tasks while wearing the same outdated lenses can be daunting. Change threatens the powers that be in institutions and social systems. Freedom of thought and true, open dialogue frequently generate fear. When you perturb a system, the outcome cannot be controlled.

The willingness to examine our personal and collective paradigms is a critical facet of being a healing presence. Suspending our assumptions takes courage. The increased awareness will help us to choose those paradigms in which all can live and breathe.

Reflections

What personal paradigms do you hold with regard to your self, your family, your friendships, work, and community?

What do these paradigms help you to see and do?

What do they conceal and prevent you from doing?

Practices

Practice breaking through a paradigm of fear and suspicion that you operate from. If you are afraid of driving on the beltway, do so this week—even if it is at 6:00am on a Sunday morning. Give a friend the benefit of the doubt. Call them again; even it has been a week since you asked them to call you. Create an opportunity to find common ground with a neighbor who doesn't say hello to you.

Over the next month, question or challenge an existing paradigm in your family, work, or community life. Let's go the beach this year, not the mountains! How about staff meetings when we need them, rather than automatically scheduled every week? Let's talk to the owners of that vacant lot—maybe we can plant a community garden.

Devote a period of time to journaling. Create a list of collective paradigms that directly influence your life. (i.e. democracy, the *free* market, the *private* sector, the energy *shortage*). What do these paradigms highlight? What do they place in the shadows?

WIND AND WATER

Take care to create environments which support healing. Create a lively dance with the colors, sounds, smells, and feel of what surrounds you.

If you were to design the perfect home or workspace for yourself, what would it be like? Would it be small and cozy or spacious and airy? What kind of materials would you include—bricks, wood, metal, glass, fabrics? What colors would surround you? What kind of and how much light would there be? What sounds would you hear? What smells would be present? What would the temperature be like?

The qualities represented in the shapes, forms, and textures around us greatly contribute to our sense of beauty, comfort, and safety. Each of us responds differently to the ten thousand sights, sounds, smells, tastes, and textures in the world.

Over the last century we have learned a great deal about the impact our human footprint has made on the environment. Less understood is how our physical surroundings, both natural and man-made, impact us. From the proximity of flowing water, down to the landscaping of our yard and the shape of the dinner table, we are influenced by and respond to the many accumulations (forms) around us.

A rapidly growing body of books in English center around the Chinese art of placement, also called Feng Shui. I would be remiss not to mention it in a discussion of the Four since it epitomizes the importance of material *and* immaterial forms in our lives.

The arrangement of chairs in your living room is one example of form and it can affect the quality of connections made among your guests. The design of a graduate degree program (via a standard framework, an executive format, or an on-line offering) will shape the population of students attracted to the program. And, guaranteed, the life of a community changes when soccer fields replace the open meadows.

A healing presence cares for the surrounding environment in the same way one would tend to a friend. Distinctions fade between what we would label animate and inanimate. All facets of the One receive equal care and respect.

Reflections

Where do you feel most at home in nature? Are you drawn to the wide-open vistas or head for the canopy of trees along the stream? Do you head for the beach or the mountains to "get away"? What nourishes you in these environments?

Review the questions in the first paragraph of this chapter. How might you bring some of these qualities (colors, textures, light, sounds, shapes) into your current work environment or home?

Practices

Observe the relationship you have with material objects around you. Do you throw them around with abandon, neglect them, or handle them with care and respect? How do they respond in return?

There is at least one physical space around you that you would call a mess. Create some empty space by recycling or throwing out what is no longer needed, then organizing what remains. How does the space feel different? Describe the changes in your practice log.

Browse your local bookstore or library for books on Feng Shui. Take one or two ideas you're drawn to and apply them to a space in your home or workplace. Take note of how the space feels different. How do you and other people act or respond differently?

8

LIFE AS NATURE—FIVE

One touch of nature makes the whole world kin.

—William Shakespeare

To be a healing presence is to know and accept change as a constant in life. For example, I have been excited for months on end about writing this book. Sitting down today, however, I am struggling to stay motivated. When I woke up this morning, I noticed the muscles in my back were tight. Now I feel them loosening. An hour ago I wasn't hungry, now I can hear my stomach rumbling. Regarding our desire to hold on to any particular experience, thought, mood, moment, or person: unceasing change is the order of the day.

What are the common elements in the ceaseless flux that is life? How do we align ourselves with the visible and invisible movements constantly taking place in and around us? Thousands of years ago the Chinese people turned to Nature and found in her a powerful and profound teacher.

Nature speaks a universal language easily understood by people all over the world. The movements and phases of Nature can be used to describe and assess how life unfolds in any living being and system; be it a human being, relationship, family, work place, community, nation, ecosystem, or planet. In the Chinese wisdom tradition, these movements are called the Wu Hsing—translated as the five phases, movements, elements, changes, or actions. The five phases are water, wood, fire, earth, and metal. You could picture them as five circles set around the circumference of a larger circle. All living things go through each phase and contain each phase in its being. Throughout the remainder of the book, I will present them in this same order for ease of learning. The Five offer a fresh and powerful way to understand and embrace change.

This section focuses on each phase of the Wu Hsing in detail. After an introductory chapter, one chapter explores each of the five phases. These chapters outline the gifts, capacities, and qualities represented by each phase and its corresponding season.

Each chapter also offers guidelines on how to embody the gifts of the phase using your voice, posture, gestures, and touch. A little background will help you grasp how these skills will enhance your ability as a healing presence.

Years ago an acupuncture patient of mine was sharing concerns she had about breaking up with her girlfriend. She was clear that ending the relationship was the right thing to do. At the same time, she feared she would crumble and relent if faced with the least bit of resistance.

I asked the woman to sit upright in her chair with her feet flat on the ground. I amplified her strength by supporting her lower back with my hand. With my encouragement, she began to speak the words she wanted to say to her girlfriend.

In assuming this posture, everything about the patient changed. Her eyes became more focused, her diaphragm relaxed, her breathing deepened. Her voice became stronger and more resonant. Her mood changed from one of trepidation to one of strength and resolve.

The patient was beaming when she arrived for her next visit. Having assumed a similar posture and demeanor in the presence of her girlfriend, this woman was successful in communicating her resolve to bring the relationship to an end.

What difference does posture make? To answer that question, take a moment and try an experiment. Lean way back in your chair with your legs fully stretched out in front of you. Open your legs slightly and let your feet splay out to the side. Let your arms relax, making room between your upper arms and torso. Maybe even clasp your hands behind your head. Put a big smile on your face. Without changing anything in your posture, try talking out loud about something you're really angry about. What do you notice?

Try another version. Lean forward on your chair so your weight is in front of your sit bones. Put your elbows on your thighs just above your knees. Drop your head down. Droop your shoulders. Without changing anything in your posture, try talking out loud about something that brings you great joy and happiness. How did it go?

The story of my patient and these two examples raise important questions. How is posture related to our feelings, moods, attitudes, and frame of mind? Are posture and physiology strongly connected? By changing our physical stance, can we change our feelings, mood, attitude, and frame of mind? I say we can.

This is not new thinking. Several Eastern religious traditions practice mudras; assuming specific physical postures and gestures that call forth distinct qualities and states of being. The observations they made can be taken one step further and applied to the realm of healing.

A healing presence learns to evoke, amplify and transmit distinct qualities of being through voice, posture, gestures, and touch. With time and practice, the whole body becomes an instrument through which we can convey intention.

There are two good reasons to learn how to embody the gifts of the seasons and phases. First, it provides an excellent way to energetically align ourselves with the person with whom we are speaking. In other words, this process can be used to create and maintain rapport. We may not understand the words being used by another, yet we can place ourselves in the same energetic boat in which they sit. Embodying the five phases offers a unique way to create powerful connections with others and give them a strong experience of being heard.

Second, we can become that which is needed via our voice, posture, gestures and touch. We can *be* warmth, humor, and lightness, *be* the calm and quiet, *be* power and courage. Our body becomes a living reminder of that which another has forgotten.

You already embody the gifts of the seasons and phases when you are with others. If I was to video your conversations over the course of a day, you would be quite surprised to see and hear how much you are already doing this work. The challenge now is to do it consciously, when you feel it would serve the life showing up around you.

Consciously working with voice, posture, and gestures is not unlike using new muscles when beginning an exercise regime. Your Gremlin will be very vocal, "You're not being real. This feels awkward. This isn't natural." Trust that with time these ways of creating rapport will become second nature.

Five symbolizes the naturally occurring movements of life. Like the Two, Three and Four; Five is yet another way to speak of the One.

THE WU HSING

*Like a farmer tending his crops, provide that which allows life to flourish. You already carry medicine in your being and always have something to offer. Come to know that **you** are the gift.*

Twenty years ago, when I first began my studies of acupuncture and the Chinese wisdom traditions, I held the Wu Hsing as a wonderful series of metaphors. "I *resemble* the energy of wood. I send roots down *like* a tree. I can bend and bow *like* the young willow." While holding the phases and seasons as metaphors, something still felt missing. Then one day I realized I was no longer speaking about the Wu Hsing as metaphors. I was speaking about them as embodied qualities in me. "I *am* the wood. I *contain* roots. I *am* the young willow bending and bowing." The potency of the Wu Hsing came alive inside me.

This epiphany highlights the enormous power of the Wu Hsing. Depending on your comfort level it can be approached, understood, and worked with in literal terms, as metaphors, symbols, and archetypes. In the next five pieces, my writing moves back and forth between these approaches. I invite and challenge you to explore and engage the five phases on each of these levels. Doing so will greatly enrich and accelerate your learning.

In the old days, I would have written that we are a part of Nature, and Nature is a part of us. Now I am more direct: We are Nature. There is no separation. What takes place "outside" also takes place "inside". In becoming a rigorous observer of how life unfolds in Nature you will become a skillful observer of how life unfolds in yourself and all living systems.

The seasons of life—the natural cycles of birth, growth, maturation, decline and death—can be observed across all domains. All living creatures have a time of birth. All families experience times of growth. Friendships mature with time. Every business venture, institution, and community goes through periods of decline. And ultimately all things in creation will share the same fate—a time of dying and death.

The Wu Hsing expresses itself through a series of correspondences. The five seasons, for example, correspond to each of the five phases. What, you didn't know there are five seasons? You will find it helpful to hold the correspondences as distinct gifts, capacities, and qualities of being that each of us possess and can be brought to bear in any situation.

Similar to the One, Two, Three, and Four, consider the five phases as jewels with many facets. Give yourself time to imagine and explore how all the pieces fit together. If a particular quality of a season or phase doesn't immediately make sense to you, just let it be for now. That I still find myself learning new perspectives after twenty years speaks to the breadth and depth of this wisdom tradition. Nature's lessons are boundless.

Another layer of understanding the Wu Hsing reflects the distinctly human functions within each phase that are collectively called the Twelve Officials. Worthy of a book unto themselves, brief descriptions of the Officials can be found in Appendix B.

The Wu Hsing is an elegant expression of palingenesis: the intrinsic ability of life to regenerate itself, to give birth to new life over and over again. Whether we are struggling with a demanding child, creating teamwork within an organization, or rebuilding a country, the Wu Hsing offers us powerful ways to breathe life back into life.

Reflections

How much do you know of the natural environment around you—the weather patterns, geology, and varieties of plant and animal life? Where does your water come from?

What steps might you take to become more connected to the environment in which you live?

Practices

Nature is the most generous teacher you will ever find. You never need to make an appointment to see her! She makes herself available 24 hours a day, 7 days a week. There are no registration fees or tuition, no textbooks, and no supplies to purchase in order to take her classes.

Choose a place in nature that you are fond of and can easily reach. Then make regular visits to this place over a cycle of seasons. Open your senses and note the phenomena you receive through them—what is there to see, hear, smell, taste and touch? Note what appears to stay the same and what changes from visit to visit. Write down, record, paint, or draw your impressions each time. What are you learning about Nature, about yourself, about life?

Before reading the next five chapters, take one or more of the Wu Hsing (water, wood, etc.) and write about it in literal terms, as a metaphor, as a symbol, as an archetypal theme. Be sure to include all the ways the element shows up in you. Are you beginning to appreciate the usefulness of the Wu Hsing?

WINTER AND THE WATER PHASE

Be fearless. Travel to your depths. Explore the places of darkness and the unknown. Sit still. Be quiet. In your presence a person will know: here is someone who listens.

The days are short, the shadows grow, and temperatures continue to fall as Nature begins her period of hibernation. Stillness, rest, and regeneration mark the season. Winter offers us an opportunity to gather our reserves of power and will, germinating seeds of potential and possibility.

How do these gifts of winter show up in and around you? Do you give yourself sufficient time to rest and be still? Time to regenerate yourself? When does your family gather their reserves, take a break, and slow down the pace of activities? What seeds of possibility are currently germinating in your workplace? Note that even the market place has its period of hibernation, which we (appropriately) call a bear market.

The calm and quiet of winter call us to the darkness and depths. These are unknown and hidden places—frightening one moment, fonts of great wisdom the next. Winter provides us time to explore internally, to inquire of and listen deeply to the inner, ancestral voices. Revived by the warmth of spring we are then ready to move forward and take action in the world.

The gifts of winter stand in contrast to our religious and secular calendars. For many in the West the last two months on the calendar are the busiest social time of the whole year. We push ourselves to meet and greet family and friends, socialize with co-workers and colleagues. The social demands of upward and outward movement clash with the downward and inner movements to which we are naturally drawn. Many greet the end of the holidays with deep sighs of relief.

The winter season corresponds to the water phase of the Wu Hsing. On the physical level, Water comprises the great majority of our body's substance. As Water we are both source of and medium for life. The essence of water shows as our capacity to flow—to stay fluid in body, mind, and spirit.

Our vitality expresses itself like the varieties of water in Nature: frothy and bubbly like a mountain spring, clear and sparkling like an alpine stream, steadily flowing like a powerful river, brooding like the dark, still waters of a marsh, running as deep as the ocean. The waters of Nature and in ourselves can be calm or turbulent, trickle or flood. Known as the universal solvent, water moistens, lubricates, and unifies. Water washes clear and bare, runs hot and cold, and reflects the world around us.

Water symbolizes our reservoirs of power, strength, commitment, and courage. Knowing how to contain energy is essential to the health and well being of all living systems. At times, we must restrain ourselves to guard our precious resources of energy, will, and determination. At other times, we must, at all costs, flow.

Water represents the wise and skillful use of our internal and external resources—knowing when its time to rest and when it is essential to move forward. At times, we feel drained and depleted—one more glitch, and we will surely collapse from the effort. At other times we feel replete and bursting at the seams, like the child who can't wait to spend the spare change in her pocket.

What is the state of your reserves and resources—inside and out? How many hours did you work over the last month? If you are running behind in rest and sleep, where will you find the time to catch up? Are you skillfully tending to your money and other financial resources? Who do you consider mentors in your personal and professional lives? Do you make good use of the wise elders around you?

In each of the five chapters about the elements, the qualities/gifts of the phase and season will be joined together and appear in lists like the one that follows. Not only may you wonder how a particular gift is related to the phase, you may notice that some of the qualities appear to be contradictory. For example, *stillness* in the list below speaks to a gift of the winter season, while *flowing* and *moving* reflect essential capacities of water. As you are coming to learn, paradox makes a frequent appearance in the Chinese wisdom traditions.

The guidelines for embodying the season/phase include aspects of voice, posture, gestures, and touch. The suggestions on posture should be read imagining you are in a seated position, as if you were having a one-on-one conversation.

Gifts of Winter and the Water Phase
in the Chinese tradition

Color: Blue

Sense: To hear

Emotion: Fear

Organs: Kidneys, Bladder

wisdom	flowing, moving	generative	stillness
hidden, mysterious	the depths	reflective	backbone
containment	source of life	moistens, lubricates	power
resources	calm	quiet	courage
will	clever and skillful	strength	trust in unknowing
patience	hibernating	reassurance	stillness
reserves	faith	listening	potential
ambition	germination	determination	storage
takes on the shape of its container	resolves, unifies	holds all	

Embodying Winter and the Water Phase
Voice

The voice has a gravelly, groaning, throaty quality with an undertone. Slow in pace, not in a hurry, there are pauses between sentences. Breathing is slow and deep.

Posture

The energy is down; the weight of torso is felt low in the body, sinking into the pelvic bowl. Relax and sink the shoulders, slightly curving the lower back. Your weight is over or just behind the sit bones, feet flat on the floor. Work with the image of water sinking to find its own level.

Gestures

The hands are mostly still and quiet, fingers pointing downward. When in motion, the hands move slowly, smoothly, and fluidly, always returning to stillness.

Touch

Offer a touch with some weight and substance to it. Imagine a firm touch that remains for a moment, offering strength and reassurance.

Reflections

Is there quiet, empty time in your life? If not, how do you regenerate yourself?
Do you know how to deeply listen? If not, how can you learn to do so?
To what are you deeply committed?
How do you access the depths of yourself—through writing, drawing, journaling, meditation?
What are the sources of your power and courage? Do you know how to call them forth?
Where do you give your power away? How can you learn to retain your power?
When necessary, do you restrain yourself and conserve essential resources?

Practices

Rest your senses by doing a one-day (or longer) fast from all media and electronic equipment. Go without the TV, VCR, computer, stereo, radio, newspaper, magazines, and books. Spend time with yourself. Reflect on the qualities of winter/water. After the fast, write down your observations in your practice log.

As a way to conserve your resources, practice saying no. For several days turn down requests to help out or give of your time. Closely watch how your mind and body respond. What are you learning about yourself?

While in group settings, practice listening deeply. Listen as if you have never heard anyone speak such things before. Listen without expectations and without planning what you will say next. Notice what is not being said.

For at least a month, go deeper into some body-based practice. Whether it be through yoga, meditation, T'ai Chi Ch'uan, or jogging, listen more deeply to your body. Cultivate your strength and endurance. Use your practice log to anchor the changes you experience.

Practice embodying the water phase. Work with a partner who will give you feedback. Take on the voice, posture, gestures, and touch of winter/water while describing a time when you really felt calm and strong inside.

From this point forward, when the gifts of winter would serve, *be* winter. Be a still, calming presence. When the qualities of water would serve, *be* Water. Flow.

Spring and the Wood Phase

Be bold. Be decisive. Take action. Create a shared sense of vision and direction. In your presence, a person will know what it is to see eye to eye.

The pace of life quickens in spring. Gusty winds move weather fronts swiftly cross the sky. Temperatures rise and fall abruptly. Crocuses and daffodils appear overnight. Green explodes into the landscape. Nature pushes herself up and out towards the heat and light of the sun. The season of spring proudly displays the gifts of the Wood phase.

Spring is a time of birth, rebirth, and rapid growth. In this season, new life is born from seeds of the past. Spring portrays the power of redemption: our ability to start fresh, begin again, renew our hopes, chart a new course, and find a new way. The same capacities are present in our marriages, families, friendships, work places, and communities. The winds of spring offer us lessons in how to dance with rapid change. They remind us how life sometimes requires quick responses, bold movements, and decisive actions.

As with all the seasons, the gifts of spring are not limited to a specific time of year. Spring arrives every day, every week, and every month in those moments when it's *time to act*. You have done enough research about that new car, now is the time to buy it! Make those reservations with your friends now for next summer's vacation. Stop fussing about that new procedure at work—implement it today! You will know soon enough whether it works.

Spring corresponds to the wood phase. We possess the same qualities as the vast collection of green, growing things in the world, most often symbolized in trees. Our individual and collective roots reach into the soil of time enabling us to gather wisdom from the past, stand firm in the present, and expand into the future. Roots allow us to hold our ground, take a stand, define and defend our territory. We have trunks and limbs, flexible and resilient, bending and bowing to the winds of change. Our bark is thin enough to receive nourishment, thick enough to offer protection and support. Like trees in stormy weather we are able to endure powerful storms of change without being diminished. Our eyes are like the treetops providing a clear view of life unfolding around us. The unique components of human vision—hindsight, insight, and foresight express the wood within us.

Like the different kinds of trees, each of us flourishes under differing conditions. Some, like the willows and river birches, need an abundance of water close by. Others require less water, enjoy more sun, and need open space. Some trees are short and squat, others tall and thin. Some have smooth bark, while others are coarse and rough to the touch. Some stand tall and upright, others are shorter and gnarled. The forest is home to all.

To grow and flourish wood needs all the other elements: the right amount of water, warmth and light from the sun, the support of earth, and the minerals contained within the soil. Without these ingredients new growth may be stunted, or not occur at all.

Gifts of Spring and the Wood Phase in the Chinese tradition

Color: Green

Sense: To see

Emotion: Anger

Organs: Liver, Gall Bladder

upward and outward movement
flexibility, adaptability
quickness
clarity
renewal, springing forth
decision making and planning
vision
organizing
assertiveness, decisiveness
forgiveness, redemption
benevolence
creativity
growth
new possibilities
birth
being directive
anger
navigating
strategizing
hope

Embodying Spring and the Wood Phase

Voice

Rising up and out with an assertive and directive tone. Has a shouting quality (not necessarily loud), often ending in a "teh" sound. Shorter sentences, your speaking ends somewhat abruptly, with a brisk, clipped quality to the voice. The breath tends to be pushed out.

Posture

Think up and out. The weight is forward, in front of the sit bones. The heels are up and moving or place one foot slightly in front of the other. Imagine yourself rising up, ready to jump into action.

Gestures

Make your gestures crisp and sharp, the hands covering ground and changing direction quickly. Imagine showing or demonstrating something to another via the hands.

Touch

Brief and directive, this touch catches one's attention quickly and transmits a sense of *now*.

Reflections

What is new in your life? What are you giving birth to at this time—literally, metaphorically, symbolically?

Where in your life do you take a stand, hold your ground?

Where in your life are you flexible and resilient? Where do you observe yourself stiff and rigid?

What are the goals, dreams, and vision for your life, your family, profession, community, and country?

What steps are you taking to achieve them?

What aspect of your life would grow by being benevolent?

Practices

Work with a particular area of your life that is not moving forward. What simple act or step—it may be a small one—will get life moving again in that domain? Take that action this week.

Spend some time reflecting and imagining. Extend yourself ten or twenty years into the future and meet your future self. Get to know him/her. Ask your future self what is important for you to know or remember during this present time. Conduct the dialogue with your future self through writing in your practice log. Based on your conversation with your future self, what decisions are important to make this week?

You can practice embodying the gifts of the wood phase by working with a partner who will give you feedback. Take on the voice, posture, gestures, and touch of wood/spring while describing something you really want to do and the steps you will take to get there.

From this point forward, when the gifts of spring would serve, *be* spring. Begin! Act! Grow! When the qualities of wood are called for, *be* wood. Root. Bend. Adapt.

SUMMER AND THE FIRE PHASE

Offer the simple gifts of warmth, laughter, and lightness. Look for the divine spark in others and gently fan it into flames. Your vulnerability and tenderness open the hearts of others. In your presence, a person will know: here is someone I can trust.

The sun moves higher in the sky, temperatures rise, and the days grow longer. The spring lambs become sheep, the apple blossom an apple. In the bounty of summer's warmth we are naturally drawn outward to activities with others. We laugh, play, and bask in the partnership of shared tasks and community life.

The heat and light of summer allow all of Nature to mature, to grow up. For example, I might ask in what areas are you maturing? Is your partnership with a significant other evolving? Are your friendships deepening? Are you growing into your role as a parent? Maturing in your work? Becoming savvy about your career?

We contain within ourselves all manner of fire from the cozy warmth of a campfire, to the radiance of a great blaze, to the unending light of the sun. Spontaneous, contagious, unpredictable, and mischievous—a healthy fire within shows when we feel all fired up, excited about being alive. Tender care must be taken in tending our fire. Not enough fire within and the joys of life are extinguished. Too much fire and our passions burn themselves out.

A healthy fire at our core reveals itself through the presence of deep abiding joys. Fire corresponds to the lightness of being and reflects our capacity to love, laugh, and play. Fire illuminates, permeates, and emanates outward allowing us to touch and be touched by everyone and everything around us. Laughter and humor are universal sparks igniting connection and communication with others.

How are these aspects of fire within you? When is the last time you had a good belly laugh? When was the last time you made others laugh? Are you good at playing the fool? Telling a good joke? Lighting up the room?

Appropriate fire attracts and draws others near, and is synonymous with our degree of intimacy, sensuality, and sexuality. Hearts open in the presence of fire and vulnerabilities are revealed. Speaking from the heart creates a space of safety and trust.

Gifts of Summer and the Fire Phase in the Chinese tradition

Color: Red

Sense: To Touch

Emotion: Joy

Organs: Heart, Small Intestine, Heart Protector, Three Heater

joy	connectedness	partnership	expansive
passion	compassion	love, warmth	intimacy, closeness
leadership	playfulness	laughter	spontaneity
community	fun/play	protection	vulnerability
maturation	lightness	expressive	touching
propriety	relationships	authenticity	sorting
networking	trust	personal boundaries	flickering
opening up	sharing	brightness	shining

Embodying Summer and the Fire Phase

Voice

The voice has a light, buoyant, and laughing quality, not unlike a stone skipping across water—fast at first then slowing down and losing steam, repeating sounds like—hahaha, heeheehee, hohoho. Fire needs oxygen—the breath matches the light and rapid sense of excitement.

Posture

A sense of being open from top to bottom—an animated, inviting expression—eyes are bright and open wide, crinkling around the edges; corners of the mouth are turned upward into a smile. Your expression changes quickly and frequently. Your chest is somewhat forward and up—purposely exposed, vulnerable, and allowing a heart-to-heart connection. Arms are away from the torso. Legs can be open slightly, or moving with excitement, feet pointed slightly outward.

Gestures

Larger gestures, light, quick, dancing, lively, and playful.

Touch

Light and sometimes playful, a fire touch transmits warmth, excitement and connection. We are here *together*.

Reflections

What are you doing when you find yourself easily laughing and playing around?

When do you experience true and deep joy?

What are you passionate about?

Where do you really make a difference?

When do you allow yourself to be vulnerable, to reveal your tender side?

How do you work in cooperation with others?

Practices

Return now to practicing physical touch as a way to connect and communicate with others. Make notes of how various people responded. How many kinds of touch can you discover?

Make it your practice for a week to open and extend yourself into the world. Introduce yourself to people who live or work around you, say hello to people who meet your eyes on the street. How did life show up differently around you?

Sometime this week it will serve to bring the gifts of summer and the qualities of fire to a particular situation at home, with friends, or at work. Introduce people as a way to create connections, see if you can get people laughing, and invite others to help you with the tasks at hand.

Practice embodying the gifts of the fire phase—work with a partner who will give you feedback. Take on the voice, posture, gestures, and touch of fire/summer while describing something that you are really excited or passionate about.

From this point forward, when the gifts of summer would serve, *be* summer. Be warm. Be light. Laugh. When the qualities of fire are called for, *be* fire. Open your heart. Be vulnerable. Touch and be touched.

LATE SUMMER AND THE EARTH PHASE

Embody generosity, thoughtfulness, and care. Become skillful at creating common ground. In your presence, a person will know: here is someone who understands me.

The rising heat and humidity point to the end of the growing season. Sunflower heads bow and sag, looking like exhausted runners at the end of a marathon. Peaches get so juicy they can only be eaten while leaning over the sink. The muzzles of squirrels grow dark while sampling the first of the black walnuts. Late summer has settled upon us.

Late summer holds the place of the fifth season in the Chinese cycle of seasons. It is understood in two ways; as the time of transition between each season and also as a distinct time between the end of summer and the appearance of fall. My writing speaks to the latter usage.

From its peak of fullness and abundance, Nature moves into the phase of decrease and lessening. In late summer, growth slows almost to a stop. Nature takes pause. The harvest having been completed we can now take a moment to reflect and catch our breath.

The Latin roots of satisfaction are satis (enough) and factere (to make). Our efforts have been sufficient; they are enough. What do you say has come to fruition at this point in your life? What is your harvest? Have you completed an important aspect of schooling? Created a wonderful relationship with a significant other? Had a family? Built a close circle of friends? Are you able to change rhythms, slow down, and pause between your many endeavors? How do you reconnect with the natural cycles of life?

Late summer corresponds to the earth phase of life, exemplified by the image of Mother Earth. She is the essence of generosity—everything in our lives comes from her. Her support is unconditional; her giving knows no bounds. Thoughtful, accommodating, and caring, she is at once both mother and home. Her sympathy embraces everyone's concerns. Loyal, dependable, and trustworthy, earth is our center and the solid ground we stand on.

The earth demonstrates how to transform raw materials into new life. The field of the earth holds the seed, receives warmth and light from the sun, infuses minerals, and adds water. When all the elements are brought together, the green things of the world come into being.

Earth stands for *our* ability on all levels of the body, mind, and spirit to take in raw materials, digest them, transform them, and transport them to where they are needed. Our earth changes the material and immaterial substances of life (food, fluids, thoughts, feelings, information, concepts, teachings) into something useful for others and ourselves.

A healing presence has a good observer for what is nourishing on all levels. Naturally this includes being attentive to the quality and quantity of food you consume *and* true nourishment goes way beyond that. From whom do you receive your emotional sustenance? Who are the people you choose to be around day in and day out? Are you being nurtured in these relationships? What are you feeding your mind? What books, magazines, newspapers, movies, and TV shows do you take in? Are they giving you the nourishment you need? How do you feed your spirit? Are you engaged in some regular practice or activity that feeds your soul?

The essence of earth lies in the cycle of giving and receiving; skillfully fulfilling the needs of others while also taking in and digesting the world to fulfill our own. Whether it is the roof over our head, the food on our table, or the clothes on our back—gratitude expresses the spirit of the day. How humbling to realize there is nothing in this world we do by ourselves.

Gifts of Late Summer and the Earth Phase
in the Chinese tradition

Color: Yellow

Sense: To Taste

Emotion: Sympathy

Organs: Spleen/Pancreas, Stomach

centered, balanced
nourishing
giving/receiving
harvest, abundance
thoughtfulness, consideration, understanding
sympathy, care, and concern
home
digestion
transformation
holding, supporting
nurturing, mothering
sweetness
integrity
generosity
concentration
loyal/dependable
savoring
gratitude

Voice

Lilting, singing, cooing, soothing, qualities like a mother speaking to her young child. Use longer breaths, almost getting two syllables out of one vowel. Use long drawn out vowels as if written in script—*aaaa aeeeee iiiii ooooo uuuuu*. Extended exhalations.

Posture

The posture is centered and grounded, feet firmly connecting with the floor. Abdominal muscles and diaphragm are relaxed. Reflective, pondering, sympathetic quality, head tilted slightly to the side or fingers on chin. A round, embracing, and open posture, like an empty bowl or vessel ready to receive

Gestures

Circular movements, open hands and soft palms.

Touch

Like a strong foundation, this touch supports from underneath, providing a sense of embracing and surrounding. An earth touch conveys support and understanding.

Reflections

What aspects of your life are deeply fulfilling? What are you doing when you feel that way?

What are the ways you take care of yourself? In what ways do you not take care of yourself?

In what ways do you provide for the needs of others? What do you need from others at this time?

How do you take in and assimilate the offerings of others (food, comfort, love, guidance)?

How are you transforming?

Practices

Reflect upon and write about the many blessings you have had and do have in your life. Include the many times you received assistance from others. Can you find a single thing in your life that you have accomplished by yourself?

A harvest only becomes a harvest when it reaches those who need it. In your home or your workplace are items (clothing, books, computers) that you no longer need or use and would be of value to others. See that they are delivered to those who can use them.

Over the next week take on this simple practice: Give what you have. Ask for what you need. Record your observations in your practice log.

You can practice embodying the gifts of the earth phase by working with a partner who will give you feedback. Take on the voice, posture, gestures, and touch of late summer/earth while describing a time in your life when you were really taken care of.

From this point forward, when the gifts of late summer are called for, *be* late summer. Slow down. Savor the moment. Appreciate the harvest. When the qualities of earth would serve, *be* earth. Give of yourself. Be what is needed. Offer true sustenance.

Autumn and the Metal Phase

Honor the uniqueness of self and others. Discover that which is blessed and dear. Grieve for the preciousness of what you have lost. In your presence, a person will know: I can be myself here.

The light and warmth of the sun grow ever scarce. The sap in the trees drops to the roots and leaves begin to fall, enriching the soil for next year's growth. The outline of bare trees against the pale sky reveals the direction of the season—nature moving downward and inward.

Autumn is a natural time of decline and death, a necessary time of pruning that makes room for the new life that will come. The crisp, dry air inspires us to breathe deeply and appreciate the rhythm of this essential human function. Like the bare trees on the ridge, the fall reflects our capacity to bear witness and bow to life just as it is. We acknowledge our strengths and shortcomings, our gifts and wounds, the pleasures and pain that show up every day of our lives.

Like the gifts from each of the seasons, the gifts of autumn are available all the time. Every day calls us to let go—from the mundane to the noteworthy, from the trivial to that most dear. The favorite slippers you have had for years finally need to be tossed. You put down the cigarettes or the bottle for the last time. Your old college friend no longer gets that holiday card. A favorite co-worker takes another job. The intimate dance with your significant other comes to an abrupt end. An elder in the family becomes ill and quickly succumbs. In one and the same moment, autumn calls us to acknowledge the preciousness of life and its impermanence.

Autumn corresponds to the metal phase of the Wu Hsing. In the literal sense, precious metals like gold, silver, and platinum exemplify the metal element in Nature. Refined and purified into ornaments and jewelry, they symbolize that which we treasure and hold dear. We use these precious metals to mark the sacred and they form the materials of consecrated vessels. Trace minerals like sodium, potassium, magnesium, and calcium reflect the metal element in the human body. Present in only small amounts; yet they are essential for life.

The metal phase symbolizes the intrinsic value of every facet of creation; assuring us that simply by being we possess dignity and integrity. Our personal values also represent the metal, being the living expression of who we are at the core. In living a life aligned with our core values, we hold true to our deepest self. Not doing so leads to dissonance and internal conflict.

Gifts of Fall and the Metal Phase in the Chinese Tradition

Color: White

Sense: To smell

Emotion: Grief

Organs: Lungs, Large Intestine

> *downward and inward movement*
> *breath*
> *letting go*
> *awe*
> *inspiration*
> *respecting/honoring*
> *loss*
> *acknowledgement*
> *purity and essence*
> *connection to heaven*
> *dignity and integrity*
> *righteousness*
> *pruning—cutting away that which is no longer needed*
> *minerals*
> *rhythm*
> *structure*
> *treasure and unique gifts*
> *sacredness*
> *precision*
> *value*

Embodying Fall and the Metal Phase

Voice

Offer a quiet and subdued tone, one of awe and respect, a sense of the sacred. The tone is serious, not necessarily solemn. There is a weeping or breathless quality—almost running out of breath at the end of speaking.

Posture

Thin and upright, upper arms touching the torso, like a steeple that connects heaven and earth. There is a dignified, regal quality to the posture, legs and feet closer together, pointing straight ahead. Offer your full attention by maintaining steady eye contact. Be respectful of spatial boundaries.

Gestures

Graceful gestures, smaller in size, shorter in length, with an emphasis on the downward movement.

Touch

Brief in length with a very distinct contact and release. Smooth, graceful, and respectful, offering a sense of deep connection.

Reflections

What are your unique gifts, skills, and talents?
How do you acknowledge the gifts and skills of others?
What are the core values that you operate from?
When are you most inspired and in awe of life?
What are you doing when you feel that way?
What story about yourself could you let go of in order to truly thrive? What would help you let go?

Practices

There are ten thousand ways to acknowledge or bow to another—from a card or letter to a thoughtful gift or flowers. Take the step this week to offer a bow to another who is close to you. Record your observations in your practice log.

What story about another person (a significant other, family member, friend) would it serve to let go of? Find a way to acknowledge the story (write it down, draw it, do a ritual around it) and then let it go. Do so with grace and dignity.

Spend some time reflecting on and writing about your core values. Prioritize them in order of importance. Write about how they are (or are not) showing up in your life at this time. How might they show up even more powerfully?

You can practice embodying the gifts of the metal phase by working with a partner who will give you feedback. Take on the voice, posture, gestures, and touch of metal/autumn while describing something that inspires you.

From this point forward, when the gifts of autumn are called for, *be* autumn. Let things be. Let things go. Grieve. When the qualities of metal are called for, *be* metal. Be respectful. Be inspired. Be in awe.

WALKING THE CIRCLE

Build a relationship with the Wu Hsing as you would with a good friend or mentor. Walk with it for a while. Ask questions. Watch the movement that occurs. The Wu Hsing has many gifts to offer.

While living in the Bay Area in the early 90's I was a member of a teaching group called Five Hands Clapping. For several years we offered seasonal public seminars centered on the five phases. As one way of working with participants my colleague, Jenny Josephian, made five vinyl circles corresponding to the colors of the phases.

We would arrange the five colors in a circle on the floor and participants would "walk the circle," work with a situation in their life that needed tending (ex. an important decision that needed to be made, a relationship with a family member) The participant would stand next to each circle in turn and explore questions much like those in the last five chapters: Do you have sufficient resources? (winter/water). What direction are you moving in? (spring/wood). Again and again, responding to these questions produced great insight for the participants. Invariably they would realize new possibilities of how they might proceed. Over time, we came to call this process *Walking the Circle.*

Each phase of the Wu Hsing is powerful and inspiring on its own, and as a group they offer an extraordinary overview of how life grows and evolves. In this chapter, I invite you to *Walk the Circle.* You will discover a powerful process with which to explore the strengths and weaknesses and balance/imbalance of any living system. *Walking the Circle* can be used to explore your personal life, relationships with families, friends, co-workers, institutions, and communities. The questions in this chapter are samples of how *Walking the Circle* can be used to explore situations in your personal life. As you work with these distinctions over time you will hopefully create additional questions on your own. Chapter Ten will expand the use of the Wu Hsing to explore community life.

Before reading the questions below, choose a situation in your own life involving another person that you would like to explore. The situation need not be one where life is "stuck" or you are in conflict. *Walking the Circle* can also be used to deepen and enhance a living system that is already thriving.

You certainly can *Walk the Circle* by yourself **and** the presence of at least one other person will help you to stay focused. So, if you can, find a partner who is willing to ask you the questions as a way to facilitate the process. They need not provide any guidance or coaching—that way you are free to discover your own answers.

Lay out in a circle some sheets of colored paper, candles, or even symbols representing the phases in the order of the seasons (blue-winter, green-spring, red-summer, yellow-late summer, white-fall).

Start with any phase—the one that you are drawn to, the one you are least familiar with, or the one where there might be some *stuckness*. Stand by each of the five circles in turn as you respond to the questions chosen from the corresponding phase. (Your partner need not ask all the questions from each phase).

Take it slowly. Give time for the questions to sink in and for answers to reveal themselves. If you and your partner observe you are rushing through a question or phase, give that circle some extra time. (When you find your Gremlin shuddering, you know there is something fruitful there!). Go around the circle clockwise from where you began, not skipping any of the phases.

In lieu of distinct **Reflections** or a **Practice** section for this chapter, write about your experience of *Walking the Circle* in your practice log. Were you surprised by some of your answers? Which aspects of the seasons/phases are solidly in place in this situation? Which ones show up missing? What other possibilities became apparent? What effective action might you now take?

Winter and the Water Phase

What do you know about this situation? What don't you know?

Are you asking big enough questions?

Is there a deep listening present?

What are you hearing—from inside and outside?

Are you making good use of the resources around you?

How are you managing your own reserves in this situation?

What would doing nothing look like in this situation?

What action would call forth power, strength, and courage?

Is it time to take a risk?

Spring and the Wood Phase

What is being born here?

What do you see?

What direction are you moving in?

Does this direction serve your larger mission and goals?

How are flexibility and resiliency showing up?

Are there decisions that need to be made now?

How are you responding to any frustration or conflict?

How are you being creative?

How are you growing in this situation?

Is now the time to take a step forward, to act?

Summer and the Fire Phase

What are the priorities here? What is important, really?

How is the level of communication?

Do the fires of joy and passion need rekindling, or is it time to dampen the flames?

How are you touching and being touched in this situation?

Are you comfortable with your level of vulnerability?

How might you deepen the level of intimacy and trust?

Would it serve to bring some lightness and fun to the situation?

How are you maturing?

Late Summer and the Earth Phase

How are you caring for yourself in this situation?

Have you taken time to pause and catch your breath?

Are you centered and balanced?

How is thoughtfulness showing up this situation?

What is the harvest so far—the fruits of your effort to date?

How do abundance and gratitude reveal themselves here?

What more can be given? What more is there to receive?

How are you transforming in this situation?

Autumn and the Metal Phase

How are you acknowledging the situation *just as it is*?

What is the real essence of this situation?

What can be pruned away, i.e. what is no longer needed?

What is sacred?

What would an inspired response look like?

How do acknowledgement and respect show up in this situation?

How do your actions reflect your core values?

Reflections and **Practices** for this chapter have been incorporated into the text above.

9

LIFE IN A BODY

Illness is to health what dreams are to the waking life—the reminder of what is forgotten.

—Greg Levoy
Callings

More verb than noun, more process than object, more energy than matter—the human body exemplifies the constancy of change. All day long we detect shifts in temperature and energy levels, the movement of substances into, out of, and within our body—an endless array of sensations. Over time each and every body changes substantially in size, shape, weight, and flexibility.

The long list of metaphors for the body reflects the many ways we can relate to it: body as curse or blessing, stranger or friend, ally or enemy, master or slave; body as temple, teacher, messenger, vehicle, instrument, gift, destiny, and revelation. Is the relationship I have with my body one of awe? Appreciation? Gratitude? Disgust? Lament? How do I speak about my body to others?

To embody something is to render it concrete, express it in perceptible form, to give a body to (a spirit), to incorporate. Who or what am I lending my body to? Who or what calls for food, water, rest, fresh air, exercise, love, and attention?

As long as consciousness resides in, or is attached to physical flesh there will be the comings and goings of pain and suffering. The phenomena we label emotions comprise one of the most powerful (and many times painful) movements we experience within our bodies. They will receive special treatment here since they illustrate a territory in which there is much unnecessary suffering.

THE PHENOMENA OF EMOTIONS

Cultivate skillful means for riding the waves of your own feelings and those of others. Be brave. Be willing to sit with others who are struggling while you navigate the churning waters of your own responses.

One evening years ago I was meditating at the San Francisco Zen Center. Out of the corner of my eye I noticed the edge of a shaking body. It took me a moment to realize that it was a woman silently sobbing. She didn't wipe her tears, excuse herself, or get up, but simply continued to sit while crying. At the end of the meditation period, she completed her bows, filed out of the zendo, put on her shoes, and walked out the door.

Prior to that evening I had never seen someone *be* with strong emotions in quite that way. This woman demonstrated one way that we can stay awake during the powerful movements in our bodies we call emotions. When we are not aware of our feelings, our behavior and actions will tend to be random and reactive. When our observer is in place, we know what we feel and can choose our response.

The arrival of emotions is mysterious. At times, they appear to arrive as a response to a specific something: physical touch, spoken words, an action or event, a memory, thought, or image. At other times, emotions seem to arise out of nowhere. They can last a long time or a short time, be powerful or incidental.

We draw sharp lines between our feelings. Some we label "positive" like happiness, peacefulness, and satisfaction. We welcome their arrival with open arms and acceptance. Others like fear, grief, anger, and despair we label "negative". We resist, suppress, and try to avoid these movements, simply hoping they will go away.

The life cycle of an emotion can be drawn like the picture of a wave; it arrives, rises up to a crest of full expression and then ebbs away. The metaphor of wave reveals an essential component of emotions—they move! Let them move through you.

To resist, avoid, or suppress the wave of movement only slows down the inevitable. The movement of emotions will not be denied. Suppressed fear can transform into chronic anxiety, unexpressed anger can turn into perpetual rage. Rest assured, any feelings not expressed in the moment will be acted out at some later date.

To what extent do you say you choose or create your emotions, design your moods? How much might you be contributing to the longevity of your ongoing funks, bad moods and nasty temperaments? How might you contribute to creating "positive" emotions and design constructive feelings? Some of the **Practices** at the end of the chapter offer new possibilities.

Key to being a healing presence is learning to how to keep life moving forward in the presence of our own strong emotions and those of others. In this chapter, I move back and forth between applying the guidelines to your own emotional expression and using them to assist others. The word *practice* in italics points to specific actions that will keep life moving forward.

Feel the emotion.

Emotions are a present tense phenomenon. Take on the *practice* of breaking apart generic phrases like stressed, depressed, jealous, guilty, or anxious. Do so by locating in the body where movement is taking place. Get to the specific, embodied phenomena (tight throat, hot face, churning stomach, heaviness in the chest). The next time you are in the presence of someone experiencing powerful feelings, *practice* offering physical touch. Note whether and how your touch is received.

Sit with/breathe with/observe your feelings.

On occasion, acting out "negative" emotions via shouting, yelling, or screaming becomes a way to **not** be in touch with them. Like the example of the woman in the zendo, we can ride the wave of our feelings by just being with them and doing next to nothing. Next time you are aware of powerful emotions moving through you, *practice* being still. Connect with your breath and notice where movement is happening inside you.

Identify/Acknowledge feelings.

Some words we use to describe our feelings actually describe thoughts and conclusions (I feel inadequate, worthless, no good ..). Other words we use to describe feelings are actually interpretations of other's actions (I feel cheated, misunderstood, unsupported). *Practice* the use of words that describe actual feelings (angry, sad, frightened). Marshall Rosenberg has done a brilliant job of outlining these critical distinctions in his book *Non-Violent Communication A Language of Compassion*. (See the Recommended Reading list).

People often say they don't know how they feel. Collectively we have created thousands of words to describe the movement of emotions, yet we access only a very small portion of these words in our daily language. *Practice* getting to the point where you find some word to describe what is happening—be it angry, sad, afraid, ecstatic, amazed, etc.

In some situations, we often find ourselves moving quickly back and forth between two or more emotions. Anger and grief, for example, often arise together. Acknowledge each of your feelings. Know that you can feel this and this and this…all at the same time.

Accept emotions. Learn from them.

Allow yourself to be a human being. Let yourself experience your emotions, even if you do not immediately understand why you feel the way you do. Extend the same courtesy to others. Emotions are powerful teachers. *Practice* asking yourself the question, "What am I learning about myself by having these feelings?" In the treatment room, I often see patients become aware for the first time of the depth of their grief, or rage, or fear. We frequently misjudge the size of the wave.

Express your emotions.

You may or may not wish to give full expression to your feelings in the moment, especially when in conflict with another. If your observer is not present, speaking your emotions can be risky business and create further separation and opposition. Take on the practice of regaining your observer before you proceed, even while experiencing the wave.

When you are with other people who are experiencing powerful emotions, make room for them to express themselves. Listening may be all that is required. The other person may not be looking for any guidance or coaching—they may just need to be heard.

You may sometimes find that another person is unwilling or unable to make room for you to express your emotions. *Practice* expressing your emotions in other creative ways—write a letter, carry on a written dialogue in your journal, draw the emotions, paint them, dance with them.

Be conscious of your language.

Can another person or event make you feel any particular way? Probably not, yet when you say to another, "You make me mad" or "That's really scary" you place both the phenomenon and control of the phenomenon outside of yourself—in the hands of another person or event. *Practice* using different phrases:

> *In the presence of x I feel y.*
> *When I see x I feel y.*
> *When I hear you say x, I feel y.*
> *When x happens, I feel y.*

Such phrases create a very different scenario because they accurately describe where the phenomenon is taking place, i.e. in your body. They also remind you that you can choose your own response. Being less loaded with blame, these phrases are easier for another to hear and act upon.

Let emotions guide you to the next step.

Life does not stop in the presence of powerful feelings. The project at work still needs to be completed and the kids still need to be picked up after practice. Once a wave of feelings winds down, *practice* asking questions that call for forward movement. Ask yourself or the other person, "What do you want now?" "Is there a request you want to make?" "What do you want to do?" (Allow sufficient time to not know the answer before moving into action.)

Let them go.

How do you know when a wave of emotion is complete for the moment? Use your observer. Watch for the natural signs that the crest of the wave has passed: a sigh or two, breathing that comes easier, a faint smile, or a laugh might return. In that moment, you will find it easier to let go for now and move forward.

Trust that powerful emotional responses are not a "once and done" experience. The wave will come again of its own accord. There is no need to keep summoning it over and over.

The methods above provide a variety of effective responses to our own and others' emotions. What works in one moment for yourself or another may not work in the next. Be courageous. No need to run. Stay with. Learn to ride the waves.

There are ten thousand ways to be with, relate to, experience, express, and move with emotions. Choose those that serve.

Reflections

What people or events would you have previously said "make" you feel happy, angry, sad.... How can you now reframe these experiences using the examples above?

What emotions do you tend to feel more than others?

What are some of the bodily-felt phenomena that accompany these emotions?

What would it be like to choose other creative responses to your emotions (writing, drawing, dancing, painting, a comic riff)?

Practices

For a week take note of how you respond to "negative" emotions. When you are feeling these emotions, do you choose to be with friends? Prefer to be by yourself? Talk about them a lot? Keep yourself busy? Stay in bed? What other responses are available to you? Choose different responses this week and record what you observed in your practice log.

Before you go to bed, design the "positive" mood you will create for the next day. Give it a name—optimistic, calm, happy, excited, and place a reminder where you will see it first thing in the morning. Become that mood the minute your feet hit the floor. Maintain the mood regardless of the circumstances around you. Write down your observations of how life showed up each day.

Sometime soon you will be in the presence of someone who is experiencing a powerful emotion. Choose to physically move closer to them. Sit or stand closer than you might have in the past. Remember the many different qualities of touch (directive, warm, sympathetic, respectful, reassuring). Extend yourself by combining your words with physical touch. How did the other respond in return?

SYMPTOM, SYMBOL AND SOUL

Hold symptoms and illness as friends and guides. Be attentive to the soulful messages contained within them. Call us back to the whole of ourselves. Help us bear what we must bear.

Medicine in the West has fallen prey to two commonly held illusions. First, that health is the natural, ordained state of life and illness an aberration, shortcoming, or failure. We have come to believe that if only we led healthier lives, all pain and suffering would disappear. The second illusion follows from the first; the notion that illness and symptoms are enemies to be banished, made to disappear at all costs. If only it were that simple.

The Greek roots of symptom (symptoma, sympiptein) and symbol (symbolon, symballein) are similar. Symptoms and symbols are both signs that suggest something else. They are visible signs of the invisible. I offer the possibility that illnesses and symptoms are often messengers: embodied expressions of soul and spirit that guide us in life's journey.

One time I asked a class of acupuncture students to write about their chronic aches, pains, and times of ill health as both wounds and gifts. Their responses in italics below reveal facets of illness that may be new to you. Listen for the deep wisdom that arises alongside pain and discomfort.

My illness keeps calling me back to my senses—to keep watching, listening, feeling, to see what makes a difference.

Dr. J.R. Worsley would fondly tell the story of a man driving his car when the oil light on the dashboard comes on. Rather than stop at the service station, he reaches under the dash and rips out the wire leading to the oil light bulb. Problem solved! The analogy for our health care is that taking steps to make symptoms disappear while not pursuing their cause is a formula for disaster.

One alternative to banishing our symptoms is to explore and listen to them. Symptoms are often teachers, wise friends, and allies. For example, when my lower back begins to tighten up, I have learned to rest, stretch more, and take a break from my work. When phlegm begins to build up in my nose and throat, I know it is time to reduce the dairy and sugar in my diet. All manner of chronic diseases, from asthma and heart disease to diabetes or low-back pain can be powerful teachers. When we have our observer in place, we can accurately assess the impact our life-style choices have on our day-to-day health.

My chronic back pain set me on a totally different path. It changed the direction of my life.

This student had left his previous career because of his physical condition. The search for relief finally led him to seek treatment with acupuncture. Ironically, the modality of acupuncture provided only minimal relief for his pain. Nevertheless, because of other benefits he received with treatment, this man decided to become an acupuncturist.

Symptoms and major illness often initiate a spiritual journey of healing. Not unlike the mythological hero's journey, the journey of healing may require that something of value be left behind: existing work or career, a favorite form of exercise, or soulful enjoyment. Trust that when one door closes, another one opens.

My pain allows me to empathize with others. It reminds me that we are all in some kind of pain. It brings me closer to others.

All human beings are wounded; thus all healers are wounded healers. All practitioners of the healing arts are themselves works in progress. All are involved in a healing journey no different than the patients or clients they tend. Health care practitioners are quite human—meaning they have limited vision and blind spots. Most importantly there is some measure of pain in their lives, just like their patients or clients.

One becomes a healing presence by knowing that even with all your faults and foibles, you always have something to offer in your being. Having it all together is not a requirement of being a healing presence.

Listening is healing. Sympathy and empathy are healing, along with physical touch and the ten thousand other ways of being with someone who is ill or in pain. Transform your own experience of pain and suffering into an offering that serves others.

My (ongoing) pain is still a mystery to me.

To be born into a physical body means experiencing some degree of physical, mental, emotional, or spiritual discomfort almost every day of our lives. Some of these discomforts—from constant worrying and anxiety, to arthritis, to eczema, to headaches—may never be healed or cured. Maybe they are not meant to be healed. They are visible signs of invisible, sacred wounds. We live with them, bear them, learn from them, and manage our lives in their presence. Human suffering will always remain one of the mysteries.

My father's behavior towards me was an example of how not to be. I realized what he did was something I didn't want to pass on to others or my children. I learned about forgiveness.

Wounds from the early years tend to cut deep. The elders around us (parents, teachers, religious figures) sometimes teach us more about the dark than the light. Even though it may take a lifetime, the lead of early pains **can** be transformed into the gold of forgiveness.

My illness increased the closeness and bonding among my family members. It kept us together and brought out the best in everyone around me.

Illness and its accompanying symptoms evoke compassion and sympathy. We do tend to respond positively to a crisis and people in need. In the face of illness, personal differences are temporarily set aside for the sake of a larger task.

The fluttering heart, the low-back pain, the little tinges of blood in the stool, the new spot on the skin; each are like the oil light glaring on the dashboard. Yes, we can travel down the medicine aisle, searching for something to make the symptoms disappear. A Western check-up may well be wise. At the same time, we might also hold our symptoms as teachers and allies. We might carry on a dialogue and ask them, "What do you mean?" "What do you have to say to me?" Symptoms, like symbols, are visible signs of something invisible. Attend to the soulful messages they bear.

Reflections

Do you have a chronic condition that really has not resolved with various modalities of care? What have you learned from it? What would it be like to work with it as ally and friend?

What illnesses or conditions changed the course of your life? What have been the benefits of that shift?

The French word "blesser" means to wound. How might you understand your wounds as blessings and gifts?

Have any of your wounds or illnesses announced or revealed signs of an unfolding destiny?

How would you cure your symptoms or wounds if you held them to be a revelation?

Practices

Take a condition, symptom, or illness that you are currently experiencing on any level of body, mind, or spirit. Create three stories about what it means. Be wild and fanciful, using myths, metaphors, and archetypes. For example, a hot, red, skin rash might symbolize your passions boiling over in some arena or that you are being branded and accepted into the Sun Tribe. What did you learn from expanding the possible meanings of your symptom? Write down your stories in your practice log.

Take a symptom or sign of *dis-ease* in your marriage, family life, or workplace. Again, create three wild and fanciful stories about what it means. What did you learn from working this way? Does this reveal other possibilities of how to relate to the *dis-ease*?

Work with a partner and choose a prevalent condition—AIDS, ADHD, cancer. Imagine that these phenomena are actually signs from the soul of the world. What might the world be speaking to us via the prevalence of these signs? Allow yourself to be inspired.

10

LIFE IN COMMUNITY

We don't so much build communities as we are already built into them. Just by being here in the world our life is with others.

—James Hillman
Rag and Bone Shop of the Heart

From the moment we slid from the birth canal into an expectant group of tenders, we have lived in family and community. To thrive in our journey we require many gifts from others: direction, love, companionship, understanding, respect, and wisdom. I hold community to be a necessity, not a luxury. The lack of a felt sense of belonging to a larger group is a great source of human suffering.

Is there such a thing as a solitary self? Is there an "I" that can be defined separate from family, friends, neighbors, work, and community life? Again we find a paradox: each of us is whole and complete exactly as we are and we are completed by one another's presence. Whether we call it being in relationship, cooperating with each other, working together, going to the marketplace, or simply rubbing elbows—all are ways we come to know ourselves.

Communities form around a shared sense of purpose. We play sports, raise money, volunteer, pray, and heal together. We gather in groups for the rituals that bind us: birthdays, graduations, weddings, holidays, retirement parties, and funerals. Through community we accomplish together what one cannot alone. In the process, we are touched, moved, and transformed.

The Latin roots of the word reveal several wonderful images of community. The word cum means together, among, or with, and munus means gift. Community becomes a place to offer our gifts to others and receive their gifts in return.

The essays in Chapter Ten offer creative uses of the Wu Hsing to explore various aspects of community life. By community, I mean any groups that take on tasks together, from volunteer activities with neighbors and friends, to team projects at work, to international organizations.

ASSESSING COMMUNITY LIFE

Tend to groups and organizations as if they were living things. Learn to take their pulse through skillful inquiry. Create healthy organizations and communities in which we can freely give and receive of one another's gifts.

Chapter Eight provided an introduction to *Walking The Circle*; a method of using the Wu Hsing to explore the state of the five phases in our individual lives. This chapter expands the process to assess the health and vitality of community life. I will use both the words community and organization to include any groups where members gather together to carry out shared tasks.

I created an earlier version of these questions in 2000 as a way to explore the health of the faculty body of the Tai Sophia Institute. The questions originally appeared in the Institute's Faculty Handbook. With some exceptions, you will see that the questions reflect those used to explore our personal lives, outlined in Chapter Eight.

Before working with the questions below, choose an organization, institution, or community you participate in that you can explore via these questions. In lieu of a distinct **Practice** section for this chapter, bring these questions with you to the next gathering of your community. Observe how each of the five phases shows up in the group. Share your observations with the group over time and create some effective actions that will enhance the life of the group. Be what is missing! Keep notes in your practice log of how life in the community shows up differently.

Winter and the Water Phase

What do we know about our organization? What don't we know?

Are we asking the right questions?

Are we asking big enough questions about our purpose together?

What do we hear from inside and outside our community?

What can we do to create an environment in which we truly listen to one another?

How do we accurately assess and maintain our reserves and resources (financial, human, etc.)?

How can we draw on the courage, strength and power of our members?

In what ways is our community becoming wiser?

Is it time for our organization to take some risks?

Spring and the Wood Phase

What are we giving birth to in our work together?

What do we see inside and outside our community?

How does the current direction we are taking reflect our larger mission and goals?

Who is holding the vision, the long-term view?

Who is responsible for the nitty-gritty and tracking specifics?

What decisions need to be made?

How can our organization deal with frustration and conflict?

In what ways can we make use of the creativity of all our members?

How might we cultivate new members and continue to grow?

How will our efforts serve the generations to come?

Summer and the Fire Phase

How do we create clear communication and partnership among our members?

Who are the hidden leaders and how do we make good use of them?

Are our priorities clear to everyone in the organization?

How can we maintain the passion and excitement of our members?

How do we communicate our goals and achievements to those outside the organization?

Are we having fun as we carry out our tasks?

How are we maturing as a community?

Late Summer and the Earth Phase

In what ways do we take care of our members?

What specific help and guidance do we need from other sources?

Do we give ourselves adequate time to reflect upon our community?

Do we understand each other?

How do we take in and assimilate the feedback of our members?

What is the harvest—the fruit of our efforts this year?

Is some portion of the harvest directed to renewal and maintenance?

How do we make sure those we intended receive the harvest?

How are we transforming as a community?

Autumn and the Metal Phase

Are we maintaining the quality of our community?

How do we show respect for each other and our differing views?

In what ways can we acknowledge members' gifts of time, money, and skills?

How do we draw on the inspiration of our members?

How can we let go of that which no longer serves (a policy, procedure, tradition)?

Do we fully grasp the value of our work together?

Reflections and **Practices** for this chapter have been incorporated into the text above.

WHEN THE COMMUNITY GATHERS

Bring the gifts of the Wu Hsing to your meetings and gatherings. Consciously tend to life as it shows up in these settings. See that your collective work produces a harvest.

Let's say you have been assigned to a key, but rancorous committee at work. Perhaps you have begun volunteering, or you sit on the board of your church or community group. Every gathering in these settings provides you with opportunities to be a healing presence. You can be the one to smooth a bumpy ride, supply what is missing, or get the group moving again when it gets "stuck".

Take a moment and imagine all the hours in your life you have spent in meetings: work or school related, volunteer and fund raising groups, sports leagues, church groups, neighborhood groups, political activities, etc. No small amount of time, is it? Gathering together as one body is an unavoidable aspect of community life. The gatherings usually forward in some way the activities or business of the group, or are rituals marking transitional events and the passing of time. This chapter focuses on the first variety, the possibilities of how we might tend to life while "taking care of business."

To be a healing presence in these settings, two basic questions will set you on your way:

What are the conditions that will allow life to flourish here?

How can I be, what can I do, and what can I say to promote these conditions?

For example, we have all seen a person lead a meeting and lose the direction—get drawn into conversations about unrelated issues. The dominant paradigm presumes that responsibility for how the meeting unfolds belongs solely to its leader(s). So you start talking to the person next to you, doodling, or writing down your grocery list.

To be a healing presence in these settings is to operate from another paradigm: as a participant you share responsibility for achieving a good outcome. In operating from this paradigm, your response to a wandering meeting might be to ask whether the group is on track, or make a request to get back to the work at hand. When participants share responsibility for the outcomes, the chances of achieving your goals begins to rocket upward.

The offerings that follow were generated by students at the Fall Symposium of the Tai Sophia Institute held in September of 1998. I compiled and edited their offerings into the format below. As always, please do not fret if you cannot understand why certain entries are associated with a particular phase or season. Simply let them wash over you. These students have been steeping in the distinctions longer than you and are a few steps ahead of you in their understanding.

These guidelines will help you become a better observer, a better listener, a better speaker, and better caretaker of the group process. Choose the "treatment" that will forward the life of all those in the room.

From Winter and the Water Phase

• Offer your deep listening.

• Make sure others are listening before important issues are addressed.

• Speak in the presence of your own discomfort (also called having courage).

• Make good use of the wisdom of the elders.

• Cultivate a willingness to be beginners at what you are doing.

• Stay in the unknown as long as is needed.

• Ask the questions that need to be asked.

• Monitor the use of resources (human, financial, time, etc.)

• Claim your personal and collective power.

From Spring and the Wood Phase

• Arrive on time, ready to go.

• When it's time to act—act! When it's time to lead—lead!

• Transform your frustration into a new vision of how to proceed.

• Speak up when the direction of the meeting is unclear.

• If you do not understand what someone said or did, get it clarified right away.

• Make clear, crisp requests.

• Make sure there are written instructions for any new or complicated task.

• Ask yourself "Will this serve?" **before** you speak or act.

- When people get antsy, give them time to move and stretch.
- Speak to the future. How will this meeting serve the next generations?
- What a concept: actually make a plan!

From Summer and the Fire Phase

- Feed the flame, i.e. the passion of the members!
- Bring warmth, humor and lightness to the meeting.
- Have fun and stay on task.
- Remember and use people's names.
- Look at people when you speak to them.
- Introduce yourself to new members, extend yourself to unfamiliar faces.
- Use touch.
- Speak out. Speak for yourself.
- Allow time and space for new members to interact with each other.
- Foster smaller groups who share special interests (playing sports, etc.)
- Have regular and/or spontaneous events "just" for fun and socializing (celebrating birthdays, acknowledging milestones).
- Clarify priorities.

From Late Summer and the Earth Phase

- Bring food!
- Ask for help.
- Offer to help.
- Think less.
- Think more.

- Be good stewards of the physical space your group occupies.

- Build common ground. Establish what people do agree upon and build from there.

- Be aware of the cycle of seasons in the group's process.

- Make sure there is understanding in the room before moving on.

- Be aware of your own needs while tending to the needs of the group.

From Autumn and the Metal Phase

- Breathe!

- Be aware of the rhythm of the group's activities.

- Bring poems, quotes, readings, and teaching stories to inspire.

- Use your words to add to, not take away from another's speaking.

- Recognize the individual gifts of members.

- Go beyond "Oh, it was nothing." Make sure acknowledgements are truly received.

- Let go of that which no longer serves (committees, procedures, traditions).

- Acknowledge the special contributions of those who facilitate, teach, and volunteer.

- Call forth the sacred.

The movement of the Wu Hsing as a whole has so much to offer. Leaders will find great power in structuring entire meetings so they move around the cycle of seasons. Consider beginning with the Metal phase:

Autumn/Metal Phase

Begin by setting aside time for members to acknowledge each other and the work of the group as a whole. Encourage everyone to speak to individual and collective efforts that are going well before discussing any concerns. The sense of belonging and connection you create will strengthen the group.

Winter/Water Phase

Outline the proposed agenda. Offer others a chance to make changes to it. Time consuming? Sometimes it is. The advantage is that individual concerns get voiced early on. You are actually building consensus before you begin working together.

Spring/Wood Phase

Run the agenda. Be clear and crisp. Stay on track. Make decisions as needed, postpone them when necessary. Use the group's time well. Allocate enough time to cover all agreed upon agenda items.

Summer/Fire Phase

Set up partnerships and teams to take the actions the group has decided upon. Make all the work a co-creation. Look for leadership from within the group. Use your own influence to guide rather than direct.

Late Summer/Earth Phase

Begin to wind down. Defer any requests to address new topics. Articulate the harvest: we did accomplish x, y, and z, today. Thank people for their contributions.

Autumn/Metal Phase

Close the meeting with a simple ritual that makes it clear to all members: we are done for today.

Of course, there are always surprises! Meetings rarely unfold in a linear fashion or exactly the way we plan them. The key to this model of facilitation and leadership is consciously seeing that some facets from each of the five phases show up within every meeting. Doing so greatly contributes to the flow of meetings and the ease with which you achieve your desired outcomes

Reflections

What are your tendencies in meetings with others? Do you participate in the activities, talk a lot, sit back and observe, challenge the leadership, question new plans and ideas?

Using the offerings from the Wu Hsing outlined above, what new possibilities do you see for your participation in the future?

Practices

Take these offerings with you to the next meeting you attend. When life gets bogged down or stuck during the meeting, act on one of these suggestions to get life moving again. In what ways did the meeting change?

Consider sharing this chapter with people you frequently meet with. Explore where changes might be made in how your meetings take place.

A COMMUNITY OUT OF BALANCE

Learn to skillfully tend organizational life. Watch for signs of imbalance in the movement of the Wu Hsing.

Have you ever participated in communities or organizations where more goes on below the surface than above it? Where growth is treated like a religion? Where "lack of communication" shows up as an ongoing theme?

Until now I have chosen to highlight the gifts of the Wu Hsing, both in personal and community life. This chapter addresses the other side of the coin—the Wu Hsing out of balance—especially in community life. When any of the five phases (or the relationship between them) become unbalanced, the gifts, qualities, and capacities they represent become distorted and twisted. The greatest strengths of the community transform into its Achilles' heel. These once precious gifts now begin to consume life rather than give it.

I encourage you to identify a particular organization or community you are involved in before reading the descriptions below. Then observe which aspects, if any, show up in your organization. Again, you may not understand how or why a particular sign corresponds to a particular phase. If that happens, please do not get distracted. Work with each description on its own merit, and move on. Write down your observations in your practice log.

There are endless variations of how communities begin to wobble. An organization can place most of its attention on one phase of the Wu Hsing and not tend to others: focusing exclusively on growth, for example, and forgetting to tend its reserves. Qualities of a singular phase, say the stillness and quiet time of winter, may appear to be missing altogether. One phase can be valued more than another: getting the widgets out (the harvest of late summer) always taking priority over long-range planning (aspects of the spring phase). Functions representative of one phase might consistently conflict with functions representative of another phase: those who do research and development baring their fangs when the accountants come around!

Parallel to what happens in our personal lives, symptoms and signs of impending disease often go unnoticed or untended. Communities and organizations that function out of balance for long periods of time will become ill. Morale, motivation, and participation tend to decline. Human and financial resources drift away. Inappropriate (and even illegal) behaviors go unchecked. A pall begins to envelop the organization.

The enormous institutional scandals at the end of the twentieth century reminded us that these imbalances are very real. Community life moving out of balance can produce surplus suffering for thousands of people.

I offer these symptoms and signs as phenomena that point to a growing imbalance within communities and organizations. They are not just the exclusive domain of large institutions or corporations. You can see the same symptoms and signs show up in smaller groups as well. I offer them not as an exhaustive list, but as a starting place for a conversation within your group.

Symptoms and Signs of a Growing Imbalance in Community Life

From Winter and the Water Phase

Questions begin to grow around how the community's reserves are being managed.

The community is unable to contain itself and set limits. Financial resources are being squandered.

Critical human resources lie dormant: the passion and fresh insights of younger members go untapped while the wisdom of the elders is neglected.

The sharing of power decreases as leaders of the organization move toward omnipotence.

The leadership uses fear and intimidation to maintain control and stifle dissent.

Beginner's mind disappears. Learning is neglected. Omniscience begins to envelop the leaders (and even members of the community). "We don't need any help, we know how to do this."

Stillness, reflection, listening, and quiet time are no longer valued.

From Spring and the Wood Phase

Uneven growth begins to appear—little or no growth occurring in some arenas and excessive growth in others.

The community fails to grow downward; deepening its roots, getting to the bottom of any difficulties, taking stands solidly backed by principles and ethics.

Reactive, impulsive, and reckless decisions take the place of wise judgment oriented to the future.

The vision and goals of the organization turn into purism; a singular, consuming, and uncompromising vision.

There is a growing distance between the actions of the organization and its stated mission or long-term goals.

Members of the organization are discouraged from contributing their creativity, imagination, and innovation.

One particular way (i.e. a process, product, method, philosophy, curriculum, paradigm, etc.) becomes the only way to do things within the community.

The group's policies, procedures, and leadership become stiff and unyielding.

From Summer and the Fire Phase

The community environment shifts. Collective efforts, team building, and collaboration are replaced by individual efforts, competition, and watch-your-back mentality.

Personal boundaries are not respected and professional boundaries begin to erode. Relationships inappropriate to the setting begin to flourish.

The priorities of the community become unclear.

The strength and standing of the community come from the charisma and fame of its leaders more than the values and principles embodied by its members.

Leaders surround themselves with a shrinking circle of advice and counsel. Direct contact and communication with the membership decreases.

Constant cheerleading is required to boost the spirit and passion of members.

The joy and fun of participation begin to diminish.

From Late Summer and the Earth Phase

The needs and best interests of members begin to be neglected.

There exists a growing pressure to move forward, keep working, press on—natural pauses in the flow of work and activities are absent.

There is no longer agreement around what constitutes a satisfactory harvest, i.e. number of widgets produced, increase in the membership rolls, or monies raised.

The harvest (financial and otherwise) gets diverted, with little or none getting reinvested in the community.

The group's effort is taken for granted. Expressions of thanks and gratitude are in short supply.

Generosity of spirit declines and the tenor of the community's conversation shifts from one of abundance to scarcity.

From Autumn and the Metal Phase

Inherently honorable work becomes imbued with spiritual qualities.

Founders and leaders are held to possess special gifts and powers, while the contributions of members are discounted or go unacknowledged.

Some consumers, customers, or clients begin to receive covert discounts or preferential treatment.

Decreased members' satisfaction with the quality of their product or service, or the fees or prices they charge.

The organization becomes less able to let go of old policies, procedures, positions and traditions.

There is a growing lack of inspiration in the collective work of the community.

Communities, organizations, and institutions are yet another expression of the singular fabric of life, the One. A healing presence knows that tending to the symptoms and signs of impending illness is critical to the health of our communal life. The cost of not doing so can be enormous.

Reflections

Have you observed any signs of imbalance within the communities in which you participate?

What are your contributions to the imbalances that might be showing up?

Practices

If you observed signs of an imbalance within your organization, how might you presence what is missing? For example, if you observe that acknowledgement and respect are showing up as missing, how could you begin to presence them, to be them? If a shared vision is lacking, how might you begin to cultivate it? If communication is a concern, what steps can you suggest to improve communication between leadership and the members?

BEING OF SERVICE

Identify the core values that underpin your actions. Take care to see that the outcomes you produce are in alignment with those values.

Each of the preceding chapters provided building blocks that form the foundation of being a healing presence. However, several important questions remain unanswered. How do you know when your actions serve—that you are truly being of help? What markers are you using? How do you know when you are forwarding life and the lives of those around you?

Throughout the book distinct ways of being, doing, and speaking are valued over others. Making these core values explicit keeps the conversation honest and provides helpful means with which to approach these challenging questions. Each of these values will be described as a movement from surplus suffering and limited possibilities **to** less unnecessary suffering and increased possibilities for our common life. These words might sound familiar. We are beginning to come full circle.

I took a gamble by articulating these values towards the end of the text rather than at the beginning. My hope is that you have taken the opportunities along the way to practice the distinctions. If so, you will already recognize these movements from inside out.

Several themes wind their way through the notion of serving others. First, there is a shift in *awareness*. New and different ways of being, doing, and speaking become possible. For example, with practice we become aware that our words can heal or harm and choose to consciously shift our manner of speaking.

Second, this awareness creates a different kind of *relationship or dance* within and between people than previously existed. A spouse notices she is pointing at her husband and suddenly remembers she is pointing to herself. A father listens more deeply to his daughter's concerns about school and suddenly has an epiphany about how she learns. A co-worker accepts your offer of help on a project and the undertaking gets back on track.

Third, the movement *touches* and *transforms* those involved in the process. Those whom you serve will remember the look in your eyes, the quality of your touch, your helpful words, the warm cup of tea. A little bit of lead has been transformed into gold.

The following markers are a starting place, the beginning of a conversation around how we assess movement, transformation, and change. I say our actions serve when we move from:

Observer/Speaker

Being asleep and imprisoned **to** being awake and free to choose

Living out of unexamined stories/conclusions **to** closely observing phenomena and our stories

Assigning responsibility **to** accepting responsibility

Talking about change **to** having an embodied daily practice

Small Mind **to** Large Mind

One

Holding life as broken and disparate; a collection of separate parts **to** holding life as wholeness, a unity

Alienation, separation, and exclusion **to** connection and inclusion

Focusing on the individual self and self-interests (I, me, mine) **to** a focus on our collective lives and mutual interests (we, ours)

Focusing on the present generation **to** focusing on the seven generations.

Dependence, independence **to** interdependence

Two

Opposition, competition, coercion **to** cooperation and voluntary participation

Seeing only in black and white (either/or) **to** an ease with contradictions and ambiguity (both/and)

Destructive behaviors, hurt, and wrongdoing **to** constructive behaviors and making things right

Three

Stuckness and stagnancy **to** movement and activity

Focusing on what's wrong and fixing blame **to** focusing on what's possible, the ten thousand things

Transforming lead **to** gold, suffering **to** offering, complaints **to** requests, no **to** yes

Four

Holding good intentions **to** taking effective actions

Fixed internal and external paradigms **to** awareness of, and challenging these paradigms

Rigid forms that hinder the task **to** flexible, adaptable forms that support the task

Hierarchal structures **to** structures that promote equity

Healing by coincidence **to** healing by design

Five

Water

Fear and doubt **to** courage and faith

Not hearing **to** a deep listening

Avoiding the hidden and the depths **to** appreciating the mysterious and the unknown

An imbalance of power, giving power away **to** retaining power and restoring equity

Wood

Indecision, lacking possibilities **to** decisiveness, making choices, creating possibilities

Looking back, focusing on the past **to** looking forward, focusing on the future

Vengeance and retribution **to** forgiveness, restoration, reparation

Vagueness and ambiguity **to** clarity and specificity

Fire

Lack of communication **to** dialogue and conversation

Immature and inappropriate responses **to** mature and appropriate responses

Confusion and chaos **to** order and structure

Lack of boundaries, betrayal **to** effective boundaries and increased trust

Earth

Being ungrounded and off center **to** being grounded and centered

Lack of understanding and empathy **to** understanding and empathy

Being incomplete and unfinished **to** bringing closure and producing a harvest

A focus on scarcity **to** an emphasis on abundance

Metal

Lack of respect, dishonoring **to** embodying humane conduct

Holding on **to** pruning, and the ability to let go

Lack of self-worth and meaninglessness **to** self-worth, inherent dignity, creating meaning

The material and mundane **to** an awareness of the sacred

Our chosen ways of being, doing, and speaking are constantly creating movement and change. To be a healing presence is to be aware of the powerful ripples that move outward from our actions.

Reflections

How do the distinctions above affect your notion of being a healing presence?

What other kinds of movement would you add to the list?

Practices

Take any one of the movements above and *presence* it for a day. For example, *lack of respect, or dishonoring* **to** *embodying humane conduct.* How would you embody humane conduct while sitting around the breakfast table, driving to work, sitting in the staff meeting, or milling about at the grocery store? Record your observations in your practice log.

11

LIFE IN CONFLICT

Don't bring your opponent to their knees; bring them to their senses.

—Gandhi

On the list of life's inevitabilities, conflicts fall right below death and taxes. It is not a matter of *if* conflicts will show up; it is only a matter of *when*. Large or small, internal or external, trivial or matters of life and death—conflicts show up with surprising regularity throughout our lives.

Every conflict has a life of its own. Some are short-lived, like exchanging dirty looks with an aggressive driver on the highway. Others go on for centuries, as in the Mideast. No one can predict how conflicts will proceed or where and how they will end. Their demise can be dramatic and marked with ritual, like shaking hands or signing treaties, while other conflicts simply run out of steam.

Some conflicts sting our personal ego—they are minor irritants. Other conflicts produce permanent damage and death. Some conflicts arise out of nowhere, demanding our immediate response. Some develop slowly, giving us an opportunity to reflect upon our responses.

All conflicts share one thing, however. Buried under every conflict lays a request: for understanding, for acknowledgement, for love or money, for more of something, for less of something. Always, in every conflict, we find an assumption that life should show up differently than it does. And, oh, how we suffer! Conflicts can consume our time, energy, resources, and even our lives if we let them.

Chapter Eleven offers new perspectives on the nature of conflicts and some unique possibilities of how to resolve them. As you might expect, hidden in every conflict is a yearning to return to the One.

CONFLICT AS POSSIBILITY

Develop skill in untangling knots. Improvise. Innovate. Use conflicts as an opportunity to create new ways of working and living together.

Whether it is a husband and wife arguing about the dishes, two neighbors quarreling over the fallen tree, or nations fighting over precious land—human conflicts are ultimately personal. The abstractions of spouse, neighbor, corporation, and nation eventually dissolve. At some point in time, all conflict resolution will boil down to one-on-one, human interactions.

Pretend for a moment that we are in a classroom and I asked the class to create a list of words they associated with the word conflict. You and your classmates would call out words, and the list on the blackboard might look like this:

fight
disagreement
dispute
clash
problem
struggle
discord
turmoil
war
breakdown
shutdown
opposition
rivalry
winning
being on top
friction
pain
misunderstanding
anger
frustration
disappointment
sadness
fear
hostility

> *aggression*
> *violence*
> *retribution*
> *revenge*
> *suffering*

Are you tempted to skip this chapter? The list looks so familiar, so hopeless, so inevitable. We tend to associate conflict with pain and suffering, darkness and difficulty.

Yet the same word conflict can also call forth worlds of hope. Conflict is also associated with:

> *possibility*
> *opportunity*
> *opening*
> *wake-up call*
> *challenge*
> *vision*
> *creativity*
> *originality*
> *invention*
> *ingenuity*
> *passion*
> *spirit*
> *excitement*
> *partnership*
> *trust*
> *communication*
> *sympathy*
> *understanding*
> *transformation*
> *respect*
> *integrity*
> *principles*
> *values*
> *commitment*
> *courage*
> *determination*
> *perseverance*

change
agreement
accord
resolution
restoration
unity
harmony
peace

In reading this list, you may have noticed that you feel a bit lighter, as these words offer some very different assumptions about conflict. They call forth a much more spacious world.

As you know by now, there are at least ten thousand ways to respond to the presence of conflict. The headings below reflect the most common tendencies, along with a way to flip each one to the hopeful side. The responses may seem to apply only to individuals in conflict with each other, yet families, corporations, organizations, institutions, communities, and nations react in much the same way.

Ignoring/Avoiding

The classic response: don't return the phone call, ignore the e-mail, or just keep on walking. Proceed as if the other had never spoken (or written, or whatever) and hope the conflict will go away.

How about asking some questions instead? "I'm confused about what you said (or did). Can you tell me more about what you want?" "Are we in agreement here?"

Retreating

The variations are endless! Leave the room. Slam the door. Shut down. Go numb. Stop listening. Stop speaking. Offer the cold shoulder. Give the silent treatment.

Instead, what would it be like to energetically stay present (i.e. stay in the room)? How about sitting down for a moment and taking a few breaths. Once you have gathered yourself and regained your observer, then you are ready to address the conflict.

Denying

You don't have a conflict, right? You're feeling just fine. Meanwhile your jaw is clenched, your face is getting red, and your fingers are forming fists.

Instead, how about acknowledging the obvious? "Something is up." "What's going on here, let's sit down and talk about it." In the long run, denial increases unnecessary suffering. The longer an individual, institution, community, or nation denies the presence of a conflict, the greater the potential for harm.

Blaming

"This is all your fault. If only you would have." And if blaming the other side in a conflict isn't quite your cup of tea, you can always blame yourself; turn yourself into the fall guy. "Oh, if only I had."

What about leaving blame out of it altogether? Let go of who is right and who is wrong. Instead, here we are and clearly we have a disagreement. "Tell me more about your concerns."

Trivializing

Make fun of the other, be sarcastic, raise your arms up in disbelief—you can't be serious! Often used by corporations and governments, yet also available to bosses, spouses, parents, and friends.

How about trusting that there is a legitimate desire or unmet need underneath the other's position? "What are you pointing to here?" "I'm not quite getting it yet"

Diverting

Work late, drink hard, aimlessly surf the Net. Get hysterical, defensive, criticize the other side, bring up every past offense and grievance—any tactic you can think of to throw the other side off.

As the twenty first century unfolds, we bear witness to several nations that have been in conflict on and off for centuries. Much attention is placed on what happened yesterday, last week, last year, ten years ago, while more innocents die today in the streets. Endless attempts at clarifying history can, in themselves, become a diversion

Instead, what would it be like to engage in a conversation about the future we will create together? What will tomorrow look like, sound like, and feel like? What kind of world do we say will exist for our children and grandchildren?

Hopelessness

"Forget it!" "It's not worth the effort." "It's always been this way." "Nothing's ever going to change."

You are forgetting the power of your words. If you say it is not worth the effort, then it isn't. If you say nothing will ever change, most likely it never will. The antidote to hopelessness is your *declaration*. By your declaration, new possibilities have a chance to come into being.

Reflections

What phenomena inform you that you have a conflict going on, either inside yourself or with another? Does your stomach ache? Head hurt? Do you crave sweets? Lie awake at night? Have bad dreams?

What conflicts are present in your life right now—in yourself, in the home, with a friend, in the workplace?

Practices

Conflicts rarely arise from a single factor or incident. Their roots are a tangle of misunderstandings, misinterpretations, and flat-out differences in any of the following:

needs	feelings	desires	values	religions	resources
goals	plans	viewpoints	opinions	intentions	visions
purposes	tasks	truths	priorities	beliefs	ethics
morals	principles	meanings	powers	ambitions	commitments
actions	judgments	identities			

Do some writing in your practice log around a current conflict in your life. From the list above, clarify whether there are differences in needs, feelings, values, goals, etc. or some combination thereof. Create three steps you might take to help resolve this conflict, to get life moving again. Take one of those steps this week.

Sometime this week a new conflict (large or small) will arise in your life. Work with this conflict as an opening or a request, a possibility for positive change. Either take steps to resolve this conflict within 24 hours or let it go. Record what you learned as the process unfolded.

PRINCIPLES OF ENGAGEMENT

Underneath the appearance of conflict lies a yearning to return to the One. Trust that you have something to offer no matter the circumstances. Study the art of conflict resolution.

We are immersed in a popular culture that portrays aggression and violence as the primary means of resolving disputes. Within this culture, most of us have had few (if any) role models who were truly skillful in resolving conflicts. Adding to our challenge is a lack of any formal training in conflict resolution

I offer the following principles as a place to begin. The word *practice* in italics points to specific actions you can take to keep life moving forward in the presence of conflicts. Come from beginner's mind. Be willing to practice and, at times, not achieve the outcomes you desired. Trust that you will become more skillful. The world is in desperate need of those who can be a healing presence when life starts to heat up.

Conflicts are a normal and necessary part of life.

Friction between forces in the natural world produces a variety of phenomena from hurricanes, tornadoes, and earthquakes to mountains and beaches. Any process, task, or relationship involving two or more people will also produce friction.

Conflicts in the human domain are naturally occurring movements that free up stagnant energy that has accumulated over time. Health in marriages, families, the workplace, etc. is not synonymous with the absence of conflict. Conflicts will arise in each of these domains and within healthy relationships the participants take steps to deal with them directly.

Take on the *practice* of listening and looking for changes in voice, posture, and gestures that may signal an impending conflict. The voice may speed up or slow down, get louder or sometimes drop to a whisper. Some folks will abruptly go silent. Do you notice changes in posture? Does the other's body seem to shrink or draw itself in, or do they get bigger and stiffer, as if preparing to defend themselves? Do they turn their body away from you? Look for slight changes in facial coloring and expressions (the furrowed brow, the quizzical look). Do the person's gestures change—get choppy, agitated, or start to move faster?

These changes in voice, posture, and gesture *always* signal an energetic shift of some kind and *sometimes* signal discomfort, upset, and impending conflict. Take the opportunity right then and there to find out what is happening. Ask the other person what they are thinking and feeling. Tending to a conflict when it first arises accelerates the process of reconciliation.

Conflicts are signs that life is already on the move.

Conflicts are not signs that a change is needed or about to take place. It means that change has already begun to take place. Life is already on the move. The unspoken is being spoken, that held in the depths is rising to the surface, and the hidden is now becoming visible.

How exciting! This is a good thing! An unacknowledged conflict is painful; acknowledging that a conflict exists is the first step in resolving it. Now you have something to work with, new ways of being, doing, and speaking have room to come forth.

Listen for the hidden request within every conflict. The other party has a passion for some aspect of life to be different than it is. Do they want more of something—money, attention, respect, help, or the last piece of pie? Do they want less of something—sarcasm, criticism, bad jokes, or clothes left on the floor? Do they want a quality of life to change—where you spend your summer vacation, the temperature in the office, or the number of parks in your neighborhood? Knowing what is being asked for (desired or needed) makes it easier to respond with clarity.

Conflicts arise from our speaking.

I challenge you to identify any conflict on the stage of world history that was not preceded by someone's words. Some form of speaking precedes almost every punch thrown, slap landed, shooting, knifing, bombing, act of terrorism, and war. Conflicts center around stories: our version about what happened, who is to "blame" (not us, of course), and what ought to be done (our solutions would be just fine). When we stop using our words, the violence often escalates.

Take on the *practice* of being mindful of your words. Know that they might be contributing to impending conflicts. Are you describing phenomena, or have you created a story—one that might be inaccurate? Be aware of your intention while speaking. Do you want to make light of something, provoke, incite, be thoughtful, respectful, reassure?

Every conflict is unique. All participants are beginners.

The complexity of issues, the distinct moment in time, and the mix of participants always create a unique situation. No single, sure-fire method will always succeed. What worked yesterday with a co-worker may not work with your child today. We must learn a variety of methods for resolving conflict. Specific tools and techniques increase our flexibility and skillfulness.

You can *practice* using the word "I" when in conflict. Emphasize **your** values, needs, and desires rather than criticizing the other side. Let go of the need to punish another for some perceived wrongdoing. In addition, collapsing past conflicts into the current one only muddies the waters. Who forgot to clean out the basement last week is separate from whose in-laws you will be seeing for the holidays.

See if you can put boundaries around the *content* of a conflict. Do so by staying focused on the conflict and not the person with the conflict. Direct the conversation to the present moment and future possibilities.

All previous hurt feelings, wounds, and unfinished business need not be healed or brought to closure before **this** conflict can be resolved. *Practice* letting go of wanting to balance the ledger from yesterday, last week, or ten years ago. Otherwise, you will rarely find your way home.

Be an example of humane conduct while resolving conflicts.

Tempers flare, voices rise, and hurtful words begin to fly. Ironically, when we are most in need of others to help us out we move to private quarters. Quarreling parents retreat to the bedroom so children won't hear them argue. The difficult meeting at work takes place behind closed doors. World leaders meet in private to resolve conflicts that affect millions. How might we turn that process upside down? Can we find a way to bring the presence of community into the process?

Take on the *practice* of imagining that your parents, children, friends, neighbors, and co-workers are actually present, listening and watching as you resolve your conflict. Imagine this changing how you behave in the conflict. Let it change what you say and how you say it. Act "as if" and "as though" others are in the room. Doing so will bring out the best and highest in yourself while moving through the conflict at hand.

Resolving conflicts is an act of creation.

In *To Come to Life More Fully*, John Sullivan does a wonderful job of comparing Eastern and Western worldviews in relation to ideal, defect, and remedy. For example, in the West, the present conditions of conflict (i.e. what is) would represent a defect, and the ideal (what ought to be) is usually found in the future. A certain striving and effort need to take place before a remedy can be achieved.

The Eastern view reframes defect and ideal. Defect (what is at the surface) and the ideal (what is at the depths) both exist in present tense. Remedies, then, are always and already present. They merely need to be uncovered

John's reflections guide us to work in the present moment. Rarely will resolution of a conflict come about by going backward in time (the way things used to be) or moving forward to a conditioned future (when x happens, then we can proceed).

Practice letting go of the way things used to be. Create a new future, not a conditional one. Be creative. Use your imagination. The keys to creating forward movement are already present in the hearts and minds of the participants. Go ahead. Create a new world together.

A successful resolution of a conflict serves all of life.

Earlier paradigms of conflict resolution focused on how to win and get your way. Later models focused on win-win where both parties find satisfaction in the outcome. The news of the day informs us that even the paradigm of win-win is no longer a big-enough conversation.

High school friends overcome their differences and form a posse to harass other students. Corporate executives reach agreement on how to maximize profits for themselves, yet conveniently forget the effect on employees, pensioners, and stockholders. Neighboring countries bury the hatchet and form a new alliance that threatens the entire region.

We tend to forget the many stakeholders who are affected by a conflict. Two parents in an ongoing conflict imprint all of their children. Managers in a beef with each other may cause a missed due-date and cost other employees their bonuses. Federal agencies quarreling over turf provide an opening for terrorists to move into place.

I propose a new standard for resolution—win-win-win—in which both the individual participants and the surrounding community are served. In ongoing conflicts, *practice* having both parties name all those who are affected by this disagreement. You will find more than good cause to move the conflict towards resolution.

Not all conflicts get resolved.

You would like to resolve things between you and your "ex", only to find they want nothing to do with you. A parent dies before you have a chance to heal the estrangement. The boss with whom you have been feuding gets transferred to another section. Two departments in a corporation fight annually over limited financial resources. Not all conflicts come to a satisfactory conclusion.

Resolving conflicts is not necessarily synonymous with forgiveness or resuming the relationship in the same fashion as before. Each conflict contains new lessons about how we might dance with another. The alive question becomes how best to live with, how to bear the unresolved quality of conflicts.

Practice acknowledging the lessons learned. Writing, for example, helps both to reveal and move outward the swirling thoughts and feelings that may be keeping you up at night. Let go of any previous image you created of what would make things right. The desire and commitment to be constructive may be yours alone. Declare that the conflict is over. Create a simple ritual in which you bring it to an end. Be grateful for the lessons learned. Leave the rest behind.

Be aware of your contribution in creating the conflict.

Every conflict provides us an opportunity to examine our ways of being, doing, and speaking. Was I not paying attention? Did I not listen? Did I not make my needs clear? Did I not take their requests seriously?

You can *practice* rolling the tape back. Do this not as a way to punish yourself, but to learn where the wheels may have come off the track. If you can articulate how you may have contributed to the conflict arising, you are less likely to end up in the same situation in the future. Ask yourself similar questions while in a conflict: Am I getting in the way here? Are my actions and speaking helping to resolve this conflict? If not, what will move us forward?

At times it serves to create conflicts.

In the same way that health does not imply the absence of illness, peace and harmony do not imply the absence of conflict. Conflicts are positive (and even healing) phenomena, not evil or unnatural ones that should be banished from the face of the earth.

Healing social wounds and injustices, in particular, may require that we purposely perturb and disturb: to become proactive rather than reactive in defining the parameters of conflict. Intentionally declaring who, what, when, where, and how may be necessary to bring justice and equity to those in power who do not willingly embrace them.

Reflections

Do you seem to be embroiled in one conflict or another on a regular basis? Are there particular ways of being, doing, or speaking that contribute to these conflicts arising? What might you do to shift some of your ways?

What have you learned over the years about resolving conflicts? What has worked? What has not? How will you increase your skillfulness in resolving conflicts?

Practices

Explore an existing conflict in your life using the ideas in this chapter. For example, can you distinguish the phenomena of the conflict from your stories about it? What speaking preceded the conflict? Are you being an example of humane conduct in working towards resolution? Can you create three ways to resolve the conflict that will also serve everyone around you? Take one step to resolve the conflict this week and record how life showed up differently.

There is currently a conflict in your life that is unlikely to be resolved directly with the other person(s) involved. What can you do or say to bring peace and closure to the situation? Would it be through a meditation or ritual, writing a letter to yourself, journaling? Take a step to resolve this conflict in the next week.

From this point forward, become a student of conflict resolution. Read books, or take classes to educate yourself. Listen to conflicts you are not directly involved in (you won't need to go far). What lessons are you learning? Write them down in your practice log to anchor your learning.

RESOLUTION AND RESTORATION

One path out of conflict leads to the dark forest of revenge and retribution. We concede, agree, and smile, biding time until we can strike again. The path of true resolution opens to a peaceful meadow of forgiveness and restoration. Never lose faith that the meadow can be found.

Asking questions ranks near the top of the many methods used in resolving conflicts. Learn to ask the right questions. Learn to ask big questions that call the other back to the larger picture—that which is really important in your relationship.

The questions that follow arise from preceding sections of the book. They are purposely constructed using the words "we" and "our" to encourage a sense of partnership, even in the midst of conflict. If you are in a conflict, sit with these questions a bit. Bring to the table a few of them that you feel would create movement. Sincere responses to the right questions will keep life moving forward.

From Being, Doing and Speaking

Do we have our observers in place? If not, how can we regain them?

What are the phenomena of this conflict? What are the conclusions and stories we are creating about it?

What parts of the conflict arise from Small Mind? What would coming from Large Mind look like?

What practices would help to move the conflict forward?

Are we aware of the impact of our speaking on each other?

How can we skillfully use our words to resolve the conflict?

Are we in a big enough conversation with each other?

Are we asking the questions that will move us forward?

From the One

Who is holding the Oneness?

Who, other than ourselves, will benefit from resolving this conflict? (Write down their names)

What is really important here, i.e. what are the enduring principles?

Are we being examples of humane conduct as we resolve this conflict?

Can we resolve this conflict in a way that honors the ancestors and serves the next generations?

From the Two

How are we the same? How are we different?

What can we do to maintain a sense of partnership, even while in conflict?

What are the polarities, ambiguities and contradictions in this conflict?

What is the "other side of the coin?" Can we articulate the other's position to their satisfaction?

What aspects of their position would serve?

From the Three

How might we view this conflict as an opportunity?

How can we shift our thinking from what's wrong to what's possible?

Can we create three new stories of how this conflict can be resolved (different than it used to be, or a future filled with conditions)?

What would a paradoxical response to this conflict look like?

Can we transform our concerns and suffering into offerings to the other?

From the Four

How would changing any of the following impact the conflict?

Who is involved in the conflict (using other people as resources)
What the conflict is about (drawing boundaries around the conflict)
When and *how* long we meet with each other.
Where we meet to work out the conflict.
How we communicate about the conflict—in person, e-mail, by phone.

What would a successful outcome look like, sound like, feel like?

What are the effective actions that will move us in the direction of resolution?

From the Five

Winter and the Water Phase

What are our shared commitments in this conflict?

What do we know? What don't we know?

Are we willing to be beginners in this conflict?

Is there a deep listening present? If not, how can we create it?

What would it feel like to be still, to do nothing for a time?

What would take courage for us to do here?

What are we learning from each other?

How can we make good use of the resources available to us?

How do we retain our power *and* resolve the conflict?

Spring and the Wood Phase

What is our shared vision and direction?

How might we frame achievable goals and outcomes?

How can we bring imagination to bear—to recreate or reframe the conflict?

What small steps can we take together to move forward?

How can we turn toward forgiveness?

How will we know when it is time to make decisions?

Summer and the Fire Phase

What do we share a passion **for**?

What is the larger task we are involved in?

How can we bring lightness, warmth and humor to the process?

Is trust present? If not, how can it be developed?

Compromise can also be understood as a co-promise. What can we trust each other to uphold?

Is there something that needs to be sorted out before we can proceed?

Late Summer and the Earth Phase

What are our shared concerns and needs?

How can we create some common ground to stand on?

Do we really understand what the other is saying?

What is needed here—taking time to stretch, having a short break, eating some food?

How do we create sufficient time for reflection and thoughtfulness?

How does our thinking reflect scarcity and lack?

How can we think in terms of abundance and generosity of spirit?

What will be the outcome, the fruits or harvest of this process?

How can we create a balance between giving and receiving?

Fall and the Metal Phase

What are our shared values?

Can we acknowledge this situation just as it is, including our discomfort?

How can we honor the other people and positions involved in the conflict?

What is the essence of this conflict?

What can we let go of in this moment—even if they are just little pieces?

What would a bow to the other look like in this situation?

In what ways could we inspire each other, even while in conflict?

Reflections and **Practices** for this chapter are woven into the text above.

EPILOGUE

During the first months of writing this book the world changed dramatically with the terrorist attacks of September 11, 2001. Suddenly we found ourselves staring straight into the face of human darkness. Years later, powerful waves of movement and change continue to ripple outward from Ground Zero.

For weeks after the events I wandered through my life looking for ways to digest and integrate the events, desperate to transform this lead into gold, this suffering into offering.

Being a writer it was not surprising that my personal healing began with words. I received a beautiful, untitled poem via e-mail and have been unable to track down the author. I wept over the words.

> As the soot and dirt and ash rained down
> we became one color.
> As we carried each other down the stairs
> of the burning buildings,
> we became one class.
> As we lit candles of waiting and hope,
> we became one generation.
> As the firefighters and police officers
> fought their way into the inferno,
> we became one gender.
> As we fell to our knees in prayer for strength,
> we became one faith.
> As we whispered or shouted words of encouragement,
> we spoke one language.
> As we gave our blood in lines a mile long,
> we became one body.
> As we mourned together the great loss,
> we became one family.
> As we cried tears of grief and loss,
> we became one soul.
> As we retell with pride

of the sacrifice of heroes,
we become one people.

We are
one color
one class
one generation
one gender
one faith
one language
one body
one family
one soul
one people.

We are
the power of One.

    The words called me back to my writing. I connected again with the themes of this book: reducing unnecessary suffering and expanding the possibilities of how we be together, what we do together, and how we speak about our lives.

    I hope my words have served you well. May our paths cross again.

APPENDIX A

Archetypal Figures and Motifs

The human soul must see itself in many ways to understand its single grand adventure.

> —Stephen Larsen
> *The Mythic Imagination*

Archetypes

Archetypes have been called the building blocks of the imagination. Like Nature, they provide us with the closest thing we have to a universal language. Variations of the figures and motifs below can be found in the stories, dreams, fairy tales, myths, and legends of most cultures around the world.

Carl Jung felt archetypes arise from the "collective unconscious", the place where all souls are connected. Archetypal figures seem to have an energy all their own. We can see archetypes at work in the external world and observe them operating inside us as well. It is essential to remember that *any* of the archetypes may express themselves through or around us. Similar to how one works with myths, approaching archetypes "as if" and "as though" they were real engages our imagination and opens the door to soul.

Archetypal Figures

Archetypal figures are the multitude of characters and voices that inhabit our internal and external world. Recognizing and integrating them allows us a wide range of expression and sheds light on the many facets of self and soul.

Exploring archetypal figures connects the personal with the communal, the particular with the universal. We can call forth and use any of the archetypal energies

179

in the same way we call forth the elemental energies represented in the Wu Hsing.

Some common figures include:

Mother (Great)	Father (Great)	God (Good)
Devil (Evil)	Child (Divine, Magical)	Destiny, Fate
Gods, Goddesses	King, Queen	Angel
Messenger (Herald)	Savior	The Innocent
Warrior	Hermit (Monk)	Healer (Care giver)
Seeker	Orphan	Protector (Guardian, Guide)
Creator/Destroyer	Lover	Elder (Sage, Crone)
Artist	Twins	Tempter (Temptress)
Ruler (Sovereign)	Magician	Sorceress (Sorcerer)
The Wise Fool, Trickster	Shape Shifter	Hero
Dragons (Monsters, Beasts, Predators)	Nemesis	Door or Gate Keeper
Ally	Shadow	Muse
Thief	Teacher, Mentor, and Student	Persona (Mask)
The primal, primitive	Priestess (Priest)	

Archetypal figures also include the larger-than-life images, of which birth, death, heaven and earth are just a few. Our relationship with the "living landscape" naturally calls forth many other archetypal figures—the sun and moon, the elements, seasons, trees, mountains, valleys, streams, oceans, deserts, caves, the many mineral, plant and animal spirits, fairies, nymphs etc.

Archetypal Motifs

Just as archetypal figures shed light on the many facets of *who* we are and *whom* we are with; archetypal motifs increase our vocabulary for describing *where* we are in life's journey.

Participation in a tribe	Separation from the tribe, exile from the kingdom
Annunciation, revelation	Enchanted, possessed by, bewitched
Sleep, dream state to wakefulness	Dance between order and chaos
Portals, thresholds, penetrating the veil	The high price paid for knowledge
Dawn, the rising sun	Sunset, the setting sun
To betray, be betrayed	To reject, be rejected
Purification, mortification	Hidden riches, treasure
Mortality and immortality	To rescue, be rescued
Seasons in a life	Use of gifts and magical powers
The Achilles Heel	In and out of love
Mirrors, reflections	Dark night of the soul, passing through the underworld
Loss of paradise	Initiations, rituals, rites of passage
Dwelling in, traveling between two worlds	The realm of mystery
Annihilation, dismemberment	The alteration of time and space
Eros (sexuality, including incest)	Role and gender reversals, crossovers
Birth, death and rebirth (resurrection)	Failure to ask **the** question
To steal, have stolen from	Forgiveness
Repentance, atonement	Redemption, salvation
The dance between good and evil	Men's and women's mysteries
Being pursued, chased	Weddings, marriages, covenants

◆   ◆   ◆

Alchemical transformations:

Wounds, illness into gifts	Obstacles into catalysts

Suffering into offering

Weaknesses into strengths

Nemesis into ally

Breakdowns to breakthroughs

Conflicts into possibilities

No into yes

◆   ◆   ◆

The Ascent, ascending

To break our word, not keep our promise

To be forsaken

To be unjustly judged, misunderstood

To avoid or to overcome

Loneliness

Loss of magic, idealism, innocence, dreams

Providence, good fortune

The Return

The Fall, descending

The loss of faith, to doubt

Needs of the self, needs of community

Imprisonment, escape, to be freed

To appear or vanish

Appearance of the shadow

Engaging in battle

The granting of wishes

Transcendence

APPENDIX B

The Twelve Officials

The number twelve symbolizes wisdom and spirit expressed through community, the ordering of human activities in alignment with a spiritual order. In the wisdom tradition of Chinese medicine, the twelve major organs and functions of the human body are likened to officials or ministers in a kingdom. Each carries out specific tasks in service to the whole.

Working with the officials offers another way to take measure of the many qualities and capacities we possess as human beings. Each official's sphere of influence extends beyond the physical organ and carries out its task across all levels of our being—body, mind, emotions, and spirit. The twelve officials embody those distinct human qualities we call virtues, which direct the orderly life of any living body or system.

The twelve Officials are a powerful metaphor which can be used to assess and bring balance to the life of any living system: be it a human being, a personal relationship, family dynamic, workplace, institution, community, nation or ecological system. To smooth out the descriptions below I use the literary device of moving back and forth between describing officials in the masculine and feminine.

SEASON OF WINTER
THE WATER PHASE

Minister of Deep Waters, Controller of Potency and Power

The kidneys do energetic work and excel through their ability and cleverness. This official is the generator of power, strength, and the will to life. A helpful image is that of the pause when a bow is pulled back—potency, potential and power waiting to be released. The kidney official represents our capacity to persevere: the deep strength and courage to keep moving forward in the face of adversity and trying times.

The kidney official demonstrates strength, courage, power, and perseverance.

Controller of the Storage of Water

The work of the bladder official in storing fluids reflects our capacity to conserve, to store and hold on to our vital energy. This official is our ability to maintain adequate reservoirs of energy, to set proper limits at any given time. It knows what our resources are: how much we have to offer and yet retaining some of our vitality for a rainy day. The bladder official reminds us that restraining and containing ourselves serve life.

The bladder official embodies the virtues of patience, conservation, and restraint.

SEASON OF SPRING
THE WOOD PHASE

Minister of Strategy and Planning

The liver official is the Commander in Chief, the General of the Armed Forces in charge of getting the troops from here to there. This minister excels in conceiving plans and holds the long-range vision. In the liver, lies the ability to hold our ground. It reflects our capacity to be creative and assertive, bold yet flexible, organized and orderly. On a physical level, the liver official acts as guardian of the kingdom, protecting us from noxious influences and toxins.

The liver official embodies boldness, benevolence, and vision

Official of Decision Making and Wise Judgment

The gall bladder official is decisive, firm and clear; the initiator of committed action. "This is the course to take, we need to go this way…" We count on the Gall Bladder to take the necessary steps (however small) in order to carry out the larger plan of the Liver official. The Gall Bladder finds the openings and is skillful at finding a way through. This official possesses excellent vision that extends across time—hindsight, insight, and foresight. This minister has the power to discriminate and the clarity to make fine distinctions. The Gall Bladder Minister is just and exact and not timid about speaking these distinctions to others.

The gall bladder official expresses fairness, clarity, and decisiveness.

SEASON OF SUMMER
THE FIRE PHASE

The Supreme Controller

The heart is akin to the King or Queen sitting on the throne. She is responsible for and reaches out to all the members of the kingdom. The heart is the storehouse of the spirit, reflecting our quality of wakefulness. She emanates compassion and excels through insight and understanding all points of view. The heart receives her mandate from heaven, holds the larger task, and knows the answer to the question "For the sake of what?"

The heart official demonstrates insight, responsibility, compassion, and understanding.

The Separator of Pure from Impure, The Sorter

The small intestine sorts out what will serve the sovereign—and in doing so—the whole kingdom. He is a part of the alchemical process of assimilating, transforming and refining matter, separating out the gross from the subtle, the pure from the impure. This official finds the good in difficult situations and can extract the best out of any circumstance. The Sorter answers the questions of what belongs and what doesn't, what matters and what doesn't, what is appropriate and what is not.

The small intestine official embodies the virtues of discrimination and appropriateness.

The Heart Protector, Heart Ambassador, Circulation-Sex Official

Some liken this official to the work of the pericardium. As a protector this official receives the hurts, unkind words, insults, and injuries so that the Heart is spared. As an ambassador, elation and joy stem from this official—carrying, spreading and moving the joy, love and passion of the Heart outward to all. She guides the subjects in their joys and pleasures and maintains the balance of sexual function. The Heart Protector is open, vulnerable, and able to protect at the same time. The radiance of the heart is its protection. This official says yes to joy, passion, and fun.

The circulation-sex official demonstrates intimacy, protection, and the lightness of being.

The Three Heater, Minister of Balance and Harmony

This official creates and maintains the proper temperature, environment, and atmosphere within the body, mind, spirit. We might say she creates the conditions for Oneness to show up fully. The three-heater maintains communication and connections among all the officials, and is the link between the inside and outside. She is sometimes pictured as the host or hostess par excellence, making sure all the guests are being properly tended to and made to feel at home.

The three-heater official is accepting, gracious, and builds bridges between people.

SEASON OF LATE SUMMER
THE EARTH PHASE

The Controller of Transport, the Minister of Distribution

The spleen/pancreas can be likened to a fleet of lorries or trucks distributing chi (energy), blood, and nourishment. This official shares the bounty and the harvest and sees to it that the goods are delivered. The controller of transport has the knack to provide just the right thing at the right time and the right place—be it a hug, a cup of tea, ears to be heard, and eyes to be seen. She helps us to answer the question of what is needed in the moment in order to serve life.

The spleen official demonstrates transformation, completion, thoughtfulness, and service.

The Official of Rotting and Ripening, the Minister of Nurturance

The stomach takes in nourishment and breaks it down, making it just the right consistency for assimilation and transportation. This official takes the raw materials of life on all levels and begins transforming them into something useful, that which will ultimately become our harvest. The process of rotting and ripening begins the process of replenishing and revitalizing all the materials of the body.

The stomach official embodies the virtues of gratitude, appreciation, and integration.

SEASON OF AUTUMN
THE METAL PHASE

Minister of Receiving Pure Chi from the Heavens

The lungs act as the Prime Minister; being respected and respectful, not discounting our own or another's inherent worth. This minister represents the capacity we have to recognize and honor the true value, the essence, the unique and precious gifts of all beings and all aspects of creation. The lungs represent the father in the heavens, providing through the breath the connection between heaven and earth. Through this official we are inspired and revitalized, and retain our special quality and purity.

The lung official embodies honor, respect, reverence, and inspiration.

Controller of Drainage and Dregs, The Great Eliminator

The colon carries away the impurities of the body, mind and spirit, leaving us pure and brilliant. This official reflects our capacity to let go of what is no longer needed, that which no longer serves. The Great Eliminator "propagates the right way of living and generates evolution and change." By letting go, we create an empty space in which change can take place. New life can come in. This official dances closely with the lungs official in acknowledging and bowing to the truth. He will remind us: it is finished now; time to move on to the next step of the dance.

The colon official demonstrates the necessary letting go and leaving behind that are the beginnings of change

RECOMMENDED READING

Achtenberg, Jeanne. *Imagery in Healing Shamanism and Modern Medicine.* Boston: Shambhala Publications Inc., 1985.

Bachelard, Gaston. *The Poetics of Space.* Boston: Beacon Press, 1969.

Berliner, Helen. *Enlightened by Design.* Boston: Shambhala Publications, 1999.

Breton, Denise, and Christopher Largent. *The Paradigm Conspiracy.* Minnesota: Hazelden, 1996.

Campbell, Joseph. *The Power of Myth.* New York: Doubleday, 1991.

Campbell, Joseph. *Myths to Live By.* New York: Penguin Books, 1993.

Carson, Richard. *Taming Your Gremlin A Guide to Enjoying Yourself.* New York: HarperCollins Publishers, 1983.

Chinen, Allan B. *Once Upon a Midlife.* New York: Jeremy P. Tarcher, 1992.

Connelly, Dianne M. *All Sickness is Home Sickness.* Columbia, MD: Traditional Acupuncture Institute, 1986.

Connelly, Dianne M. *Traditional Acupuncture The Law of the Five Elements.* Columbia, MD: Traditional Acupuncture Institute, 1979.

Connelly, Dianne M. and Katherine Hancock. *Alive and Awake: Wisdom for Kids.* Laurel, MD: Tai Sophia Press, 2004.

Cousineau, Phil. *Once and Future Myths.* Berkeley: Conari Press, 2001.

Duggan, Robert M. *Common Sense for the Healing Arts.* Laurel, MD: Tai Sophia Press, 2004.

Fox, Matthew, and Rupert Sheldrake. *Natural Grace.* New York: Doubleday, 1996.

Friedman, Lenore and Susan Moon, editors. *Being Bodies Buddhist Women on the Paradox of Embodiment.* Boston: Shambhala Publications, Inc., 1997.

Garfield, Charles, Cindy Spring, Sedonia Cahill. *Wisdom Circles.* New York: Hyperion, 1998.

Hanh, Thich Nhat. *The Heart of Understanding.* Berkeley: Parallax Press, 1988.

Heider, John. *The Tao of Leadership.* Atlanta: Humanics Limited, 1985.

Hillman, James. *The Soul's Code.* New York: Warner Books, 1996.

Hillman, James. *Healing Fiction.* Woodstock, CT:, Spring Publications, 1983.

Hillman, James. *Kinds of Power.* New York: Doubleday, 1995.

Jarrett, Lonny S. *Nourishing Destiny.* Stockbridge: Spirit Path Press, 1998.

Keen, Sam. *Hymns to an Unknown God .* New York: Bantam Books, 1994.

Keen, Sam, Anne Valley Fox. *Your Mythic Journey.* New York: Jeremy P. Tarcher/Putnam, 1973.

Kurtz, Ernest, Katherine Ketcham. *The Spirituality of Imperfection*, New York: Bantam Books, 1992.

Larre, Claude, Jean Schatz, Elisabeth Rochat de la Vallee. *Survey of Traditional Chinese Medicine.* Paris and Columbia, MD: Institute Ricci, Traditional Acupuncture Foundation, 1986.

Larre, Claude. *The Way of Heaven.* Cambridge, England: Monkey Press, 1994.

Larsen, Stephen. *The Mythic Imagination.* Rochester, VT: Inner Traditions International, 1990.

Levoy, Gregg. *Callings.* New York: Crown Publishers, Inc., 1997.

Mitchell, Helen Buss. *Roots of Wisdom.* Belmont, CA: Wadsworth Group, 2002.

Moore, Thomas. *Care of the Soul.* New York: HarperCollins Publishers, 1992.

Moore, Thomas. *Original Self.* New York: HarperCollins Publishers, 2000.

Nichols, Sallie. *Jung and Tarot An Archetypal Journey.* York Beach: Samuel Weiser, Inc., 1980.

O'Donohue, John. *Anam Cara.* New York: HarperCollins, 1997.

Osbon, Diane, editor. *A Joseph Campbell Companion Reflections on the Art of Living.* New York: HarperCollins, 1991.

Packer, Toni. *The Work of This Moment.* Boston: Shambhala Publications, Inc., 1990.

Parry, Danaan. *Warriors of the Heart.* Bainbridge Island: The Earthstewards Network, 1991.

Pearson, Carol S. *Awakening the Heroes Within.* New York: HarperCollins Publishers, 1991.

Peat, F. David. *Blackfoot Physics.* Grand Rapids: Phanes Press, 2002.

Poerksen, Uwe. *Plastic Words.* Translated by Jutta Mason and David Cayley. University Park, PA: Pennsylvania State University Press, 1995.

Rosenberg, Marshall. *Nonviolent Communication: A Language of Compassion.* Encinitas: PuddleDancer Press, 1999.

Siu, R.G.H. *The Portable Dragon.* Cambridge: MIT Press, 1968.

Smith, Fritz. *Inner Bridges.* Atlanta: Humanics New Age, 1986.

Sullivan, John G. *To Come to Life More Fully.* Columbia, MD: Traditional Acupuncture Institute, 1990.

Suzuki, Shunryu. *Zen Mind, Beginner's Mind.* New York: John Weatherhill, Inc., 1970.

Talbot, Michael. *The Holographic Universe.* New York: HarperCollins, 1991.

Wheatley, Margaret J. *Leadership and the New Science.* San Francisco: Berrett-Koehler Publishers, 1999.

Wu, John, translator. *Lao Tzu Tao Teh Ching.* New York: St. John's University Press, 1961.

Worsley, J.R. *Classical Five-Element Acupuncture, Vol. III, The Five Elements and The Officials.* J.R. and J.B. Worsley, 1998.

Zander, Rosamund Stone and Benjamin. *The Art of Possibility.* Boston: Harvard Business School Press, 2000.

Zweig, Connie and Steve Wolf. *Romancing the Shadow.* New York: The Ballantine Publishing Group, 1997.

Zweig, Connie and Jeremiah Abrams, editors. *Meeting the Shadow.* Los Angeles: Jeremy P. Tarcher, 1991

RESOURCES

Tom Balles

Healing Arts Center
657A Main Street
Laurel, MD 20707

(301) 776-2692

Web site: www.tomballes.com

e-mail: tom@tomballes.com

Tom teaches classes on this material ranging from 1-2 day workshops to week-long seminars. In response to a growing demand, he is now offering programs in team building, leadership, and management training based on these distinctions.

Tai Sophia Institute

7750 Montpelier Road
Laurel, MD 20723

1 (800) 735-2968

Web site: www.tai.edu

Tai Sophia Institute is a public, not-for-profit, tax-exempt organization dedicated to the development of the healing arts in the United States. This learning community serves those committed to enriching the arts of living and dying, and to deepening society's understanding of health; an understanding rooted in nature and timeless wisdom. Tai Sophia provides professional education through the three graduate programs described below as well as providing educational programs to the wider community. The Institute is committed to education that empowers individuals and communities, furthering their health, growth and transformation.

The Master of Arts in Applied Healing Arts degree program is a development of the acclaimed SOPHIA program. The focus of this program is to provide educators, business people, healers and families with ways to utilize this ancient wisdom throughout life. The objective is to graduate students who are healing presences so that, whatever their technical expertise, wherever they are, there is "less unnecessary suffering and more constructive possibilities for our common life." This program, offered in executive format, has intakes each January.

The Master of Acupuncture program is one of the oldest and most respected training programs for acupuncturists in the nation. This form of acupuncture recognizes each human being as a seamless composite of body, mind and spirit. This program has two intakes, September and January of each year.

The Master of Arts in Botanical Healing is the nation's first master degree in the field. Simon Mills, one of the most widely known experts in the field of herbal medicine directs the program. This program has intakes each September.

SOPHIA (School of Philosophy and Healing in Action). Described by one participant as a "required course in living", SOPHIA is an educational program of the Institute offered to the public since 1987. Several thousand participants have completed the program in which they *learn to become the needle;* skillfully tending the flow of life as it shows up in themselves, their relationships, the workplace, in institutions, and communities. Currently offered in a four-weekend format, the SOPHIA program is offered once each fall.

Zero Balancing Association

801 W. Main Street, Suite 202
Charlottesville, VA 22903

(434) 244-2458

Web site: www.zerobalancing.com

Zero Balancing (ZB) was developed by Fritz Smith, M.D. and has its roots in osteopathy, acupuncture, Rolfing, and meditation. Relaxing yet energizing, ZB integrates fundamental principles of Western medicine with Eastern concepts of energy. ZB provides clients the possibility of health and healing at the deepest level of energy flow in the body—the skeletal system. By working with bone energy ZB corrects imbalances, providing relief from pain, anxiety and stress while facilitating a profound experience of wellness and integration.

For the massage therapist or body worker, Zero Balancing enhances other modalities and opens new avenues of energetic and structural balancing through touch. ZB is taught in numerous massage therapy and acupuncture schools around the country. Certification is open to licensed and certified health professionals, and takes one to two years. Non-certification classes are also available.

Arica Institute Inc.

10 Landmark Lane
P.O. Box 645
Kent, CT 06757-1526

(860) 927-1006

www.arica.org

The Arica School was founded in 1968 by Oscar Ichazo as a School of Knowledge. This type of school can be found since antiquity from the Greek schools to the schools of the Hindu, Buddhist, and Sufi traditions. Arica offers a contemporary method of enlightenment employing biology, psychology, and physics in order to clarify human consciousness with modern knowledge that produces freedom and liberation. Arica trainings are offered internationally.

Center for Non-Violent Communication

2424 Foothill Blvd., Suite E
La Crescenta, CA 91214

(818) 957-9393

Web site: www.cnvc.org

Founder and Director of Educational Services: Marshall B. Rosenberg, Ph.D.

The Center for Nonviolent Communication is a global organization whose vision is a world where everyone's needs are met peacefully. Their mission is to contribute to this vision by facilitating the creation of life-serving systems within ourselves, interpersonally, and within organizations. They do this by living and teaching the process of Nonviolent Communication (NVC), which strengthens the ability of people to compassionately connect with themselves and one another, share resources, and resolve conflicts.

ABOUT THE AUTHOR

Tom Balles has over twenty years of study and practice in the Chinese wisdom traditions. His studies of acupuncture and Chinese philosophy began in a certificate program at the Tai Sophia Institute in 1982, where he later received a Master's Degree in Acupuncture (M.Ac.). Tom built acupuncture practices in Tahoe City and San Francisco, California before moving to Maryland in 1995 to join the faculty of the Institute.

As a Senior Faculty member, Tom trained classes of students that included physicians, nurses, psychologists, and social workers to become acupuncturists . For four years he served as Dean of Faculty, and in January of 2002 became a Distinguished Lecturer in the Institute's Master degree program in Applied Healing Arts, the first of its kind in the country.

Tom completed the Institute's community education program called SOPHIA (School of Philosophy and Healing in Action) in 1992 and in 2002 joined the teaching team. He has been teaching this applied philosophy in a number of settings over the last twelve years.

While living in the San Francisco Bay Area, Tom co-founded *Five Hands Clapping* which delivered seasonal programs in the Chinese philosophy of healing. After moving to Maryland, Tom helped facilitate a pilot program at the Evening School, a program of studies for suspended or expelled middle and high school students in Howard County. The program allowed students to explore different ways of being, doing, and speaking, while focusing primarily on building conflict resolution skills.

Over the last three years Tom has facilitated meetings and retreats with principals, teachers, and staff development personnel in Howard County. In 2000-01, he co-created and delivered a yearlong program for educators called *Awakening Community and Spirit in Education*. In response to a growing demand, Tom is now offering programs in team building, leadership, and management training based on the material in this book.

Tom volunteers as a mediator in the victim-offender mediation program sponsored by the Mediation and Conflict Resolution Center at Howard Community College, where he also serves as Adjunct Faculty.

He maintains a private practice in acupuncture, personal coaching, and Zero Balancing in Laurel, MD and can be reached via e-mail: tom@tomballes.com

0-595-31160-1

Printed in the United States
19175LVS00005B/241-258